HEALTHYLEADERSHIP
A Doctor's Prescription
for Becoming a Better Leader

HEALTHYLEADERSHIP
A DOCTOR'S PRESCRIPTION
FOR BECOMING A BETTER LEADER

COPYRIGHT

DEDICATION
FOR DAD

Contents

5 - Connection

Chief Complaint: *I can't get everyone to support my vision.*
Prescription: *Learn how to connect with people.*

6 - Inspiration

Chief Complaint: *My staff is not performing at its best.*
Prescription: *Raise people to a higher level.*

7 – Teamwork

Chief Complaint: *My people are not working well together.*
Prescription: *Take a relational approach to team building.*

8 - Leadership

Chief Complaint: *I don't like dealing with conflict.*
Prescription: *Refuse to avoid the messy business of people.*

9 - Perseverance

Chief Complaint: *I feel defeated.*
Prescription: *Use failure as a springboard for growth.*

10 - Tools

10-Point Leadership Diagnostic Tool

Foreword

Much has been written on the subject of leadership. For generations, people have sought to understand what makes a great leader.

For those wishing to unlock the key to great leadership, there are numerous resources readily available to help you on your journey. Walk into any bookstore (or these days, download online) and you will find entire sections devoted to the subject. Unfortunately, in your search you will find several "how-to" books that offer simple recipes. If you're looking for a quick fix or step-by-step instruction on how to be an effective leader, you will be disappointed. The fact is, great leadership will never be discovered in "how-to" books—there is no simple formula. In other words, great leadership is *caught*, and not *taught*.

When it comes to leadership, seek out resources that deliver principles, not recipes. Thoughtfully incorporate these principles into your personality, which will give you your own unique and genuine leadership style.

As you read this book, you will find key principles effectively communicated through the real life experiences of a practicing physician. I believe you will find the format refreshing and the stories captivating. As you read each vignette, ponder the principles, internalize them, and you will soon *catch* what it means to be a healthy leader. What should follow is a lifelong discovery of your own unique and successful leadership style.

Rick Merrill

President and CEO
Cook Children's Health Care System

Introduction

What Is Healthy Leadership?

After years of hard work and education, I graduated from medical school with an immense passion to begin my practice as a family physician. But I had no idea I was missing something. I mean, after hours upon hours of reading and studying, of residency and practice, I believed I was fully prepared to join my brother's medical clinic and begin seeing patients. But even after all those hours and years of diligently working to obtain my degree, nothing had prepared me for running a business, managing a practice, or connecting with a staff.

My brother and I were just like the thousands of physicians and professionals—lawyers, pastors, accountants, managers, you name it—who become great at what they do, but are literally novices in how to lead people and organizations. Like most other professionals, we had no education or coaching in the areas of teamwork, hiring a staff, training people, empowering individuals, inspiring a team, or casting a vision. In all those years of medical school, we had never been introduced to the concept of personal development. Our idea of running an office was solely based on personal experience and common sense—come to work on time, do your job, work hard, and get your reward (e.g. your grade, your degree, or your paycheck).

I soon learned the hard way that having a degree isn't enough to run a successful business. My lack of leadership skills hurt me. It burnt out our staff. It severely affected the health of our business. This is a harsh reality that most professionals face. Most of us succumb to the limitations and the frustrations that we run up against, often not even realizing what's missing. We work and toil for years and even decades, without understanding that we are grossly underprepared for our positions in leadership.

I found that just like the body's health is dependent upon good habits, healthy leadership is also dependent upon positive habits and disciplines. These include disciplines of thinking and doing—but most of all, disciplines of *being*. We incorporate healthy habits into our lifestyles to improve our physical bodies. In the same way, we should adopt healthy principles into our leadership until they become a vital part of who we are.

Your human body will not become healthy by taking one pill, having one surgery, or applying one discipline. Nor will your leadership soar from reading one book, attending one seminar, or practicing one technique. If you want to see your leadership become healthy, there is much to be done and a lot of principles to put into practice. But the most important thing to do is adopt the mindset that healthy leadership is a lifestyle—a lifelong pursuit of both personal development and the dedication to serve and develop others.

As I said before, the struggles and failures I encountered early in my career are a common experience for many professionals. Perhaps you got your degree in law but struggle to advance in the way you had envisioned. It's frustrating. Maybe you have a marketing degree, or manage a large department or company, but you aren't producing the numbers your clients or employers are looking for. And you just don't know what else to do.

You may be a retail manager of a major department store or grocery store who has worked her way up from stocking shelves. You know every position from the bottom up, but you were never formally trained to manage a team. And the pressure is getting to you, because the culture of your team is infected with drama and toxic attitudes.

Regardless of your field, your degrees, or years of experience, you will hit a ceiling if you do not develop the skills required to become a stellar leader. I know this from personal experience. Our lack of leadership skills caused us to lose staff and close clinics. We experienced failure before we figured out what we were doing wrong. And this is precisely what has led me to devour every resource that I can about leadership—not just to benefit my own teams—but to empower and equip other leaders to have the same impact in their world.

Based on the leadership principles and personal development disciplines I began learning, we set out to rebuild our teams and our business. Having seen the fruit of healthy leadership in the medical practice, in September of 2012 I began writing weekly leadership articles even as I continued to practice as a full time family physician. *Healthy Leadership* is a selection of these articles, revised and grouped topically to address some of the most common ailments of leaders. Each chapter introduces a *chief complaint* from a leader's perspective and a *prescription* from the doctor. Each *prescription* is supported by a few brief articles, which identify methods leaders can immediately apply to begin experiencing relief. As these principles are adopted as lifelong disciplines, your leadership will become more and more healthy.

My wish is that the following pages will inspire you to grow daily to become a better leader—that my experiences of both failure and success in leadership will encourage you in your failures and celebrate with you in your successes.

You may find this to be a valuable resource to read cover-to-cover, or you may use it as a quick reference in moments of stress, frustration, or defeat. Either way, I encourage you to intentionally develop healthy leadership for yourself, your team members, and your entire organization.

Will you aspire to practice healthy leadership?

Your friend,

Wes Saade, MD
Founder of WesMD.com

Purpose

chapter 1

Chief Complaint

I FEEL LIKE MY WORK LACKS MEANING.

Prescription

LAY HOLD OF A GREATER PURPOSE.

Embrace Your Humanity

Friday, 7:50pm

It was the end of a long day, a long week for that matter. Just ten minutes before we closed the clinic, I was exhausted. Having worked nearly 55 hours that week, I was quite ready to go home. But then in came a severely thin 37-year-old woman in a wheelchair, carefully pushed by her 12-year-old daughter.

I reviewed the chart before I entered the room. It read, "Chief Complaint: needs oxygen." Having never seen her before, I thought she must be a smoker who just needed oxygen at home, a sadly common situation that we see. Nevertheless, I put a smile on my face, knocked on the door and greeted the patient and her daughter. As I started asking about her medical history and living situation, I was astounded by her heart-breaking journey. I found myself profoundly touched by the lesson this terminally ill woman would teach me that night.

Lesson from a Dying Patient

She told me that four years ago she contracted a rare lung infection. At this point, her right lung was completely consumed. Her left lung was on its way to also being destroyed. A year and a half before, more than four top specialists had told her there was no treatment for her, and that she only had around a year to live. Now, acutely short of breath, she was asking for access to oxygen at home.

She spoke softly with an occasional smile. Between every two or three sentences she would stop, and with much laboring take as deep of a breath as she could. She only weighed 79 pounds. She said her lack of stamina was intense. She was dying, unable to breathe or eat well because of nausea. Yet throughout my conversation with her, she had a radiant glow and peace about her.

Behind the patient sat her 12-year-old daughter quietly listening to the conversation, not making much eye contact with me. I sensed a very deep strength in her.

I asked the patient, "Who takes care of you?" She pointed to her daughter. And she said, "I know it is not fair to her." Her daughter kindly and promptly responded, "Yes. It is fair."

I then inquired, "Do you have family? Sister, brother, parents?" She said, "Yes, but they are all away." She continued, "I do have a husband, but he works all the time. He just checked out." I just looked at her, stunned. She continued, "Well, who can blame him? A few years back, he had a spunky, sexy wife walking around. Now it's all gone."

I Am Blessed

I was taken aback by the woman's painful situation. I asked her, "How are you handling all of this? How do you keep such a good attitude?" She said calmly, "It's not about a good attitude. It's that I am blessed."

Blessed? I thought. *Blessed. How can she say that? She is in a sad, hopeless situation!*

She continued, "I am blessed. Look behind me," pointing to her daughter. "She is amazing." To which her daughter immediately responded, "Thank you, Mom."

"I have a roof over my head," she said. "And also, there are so many people that have it worse than I have. I AM BLESSED."

Now, this terminally ill woman was skin and bones, nauseated, unable to breathe, enduring the possibility of death, the pain of having her young daughter care for her, and the rejection of a husband who had detached from their reality. I thought that not too many people could have it worse than her. But she thought there were. And she considered herself blessed. And I was left to wonder, *How can she have such grace, such calm, such peace?*

I spent the time I needed to care for her as best as I could. I gave her and her daughter a hug. Then, I closed the clinic and went home for the night. But I could not sleep.

Touched by Humanity

I could not help but ponder what this wonderful lady brought home to me that night. She illuminated so many realities we sometimes avoid as humans—

the brevity of our existence, the fragility of our bodies, the vulnerability of humanity, the cruelty of life, the power of love, the beauty of grace, the magnitude of gratitude, the vitality of compassion, and the futility of success.

Yet, the biggest impact she made on me was her comment, "I am blessed."

I kept thinking to myself, *How many times have I said, truly meant, and basked in the knowledge that…I AM BLESSED.* That night, I had a quiet renewing of the spirit and recommitment, not as a doctor, but as a human being to…

> *Be thankful in everything. Have gratitude for what I have. Be humble in success. Be graceful in defeat. Be patient in failure. Help those in need. And be kind to all.*

As leaders, sometimes we think we are so important. Or, we aim to become so important…

> *May we remember that we are nothing but flesh and blood. And a soul. May we remember that what we have, we can lose; what we get, we can lose; even what we know, we can lose. May we be grateful in all, patient with all, and loving to all.*

Regardless of our age or education, our race or religion, our title or social status, at the end of the day, we are all human. Don't lose touch with your humanity. And as my terminally ill patient taught me—may we all know that whatever we go through...*we are truly blessed!*

Learn about Living from the Dying

I had been treating a young man for about six months. He was 25 years old, 6'2", Caucasian. He kept a machine in his pocket about three times the size of a remote control. Without the pacemaker, his heart would stop. Literally.

Every time he walked into the clinic, he was always mildly sweating because his heart struggled to pump and his adrenal glands, in distress, were overproducing adrenaline. He was barely alive—waiting for a heart transplant.

25 Years Old and Dying

Although I did not have the courage to ask him, I knew the thought of mortality must be ever present. Even at his young age, you could see in his eyes an old soul, someone who had passed through all the stages of grief—from anger all the way to acceptance. Maybe that was why he was so kind and always smiling. As his doctor, I was always blessed and inspired by his smile. And I prayed for his healing, for a donor, for a miracle.

As a physician, sometimes you get a front-row seat to humanity and the fragility of life, and the heart-wrenching pain of our human experience. You move from room to room: the colds, the flu, the diabetes, the asthma, the depression. You see the abused, the abuser, the hypochondriac, the addicted. And then you see the dying. You push through the ugly reality.

But sometimes it pushes back.

Sometimes, a patient will set you back on your heels and remind you that he is another human being, *like you*. Hanging on to life, to hope, to dignity, to humanity. With his smile alone, this young man communicated that he was blessed, content. I won't soon forget how he smiled throughout his entire visit, as if to say, "I am okay with everything, whatever may come."

Your Place of Peace

Whatever you are going through, wherever you are—at the top of the mountain, or at the bottom of despair—may you stop and see your world from a larger perspective. May you remember that we are all part of a symphony of the ages, conducted by the Maestro of eternity, though we may not understand why or how.

Healthy leadership starts from a place of peace in the heart—a place that feels blessed, a place that smiles and is content throughout turmoil, and a place that allows God to be in control.

Keep Your Values at the Core of Every Decision You Make

As leaders, our personal values are the foundation of every decision we make in life, in business, for our families and for our teams. As I define and refine my own values, I can't help but think of and be grateful to live in a country that was founded by men with solid, enduring core values. Their personal principles helped shape an entire nation.

American Values

If I were to list the top five American values that define who we are as a nation and guide our decisions as a people, I would choose:

- Liberty
- Equality
- Empowerment of the individual
- Rule of law
- Generosity

Since our inception, these ideals were imbued into our founding documents: The Declaration of Independence, The Constitution, and The Bill of Rights.

These core values were born of the collective spirit of an immigrant people who longed for liberty and freedom. They were captured by wise men and put into words. These and the other foundational ethos that sprang out of them have been defended by pen and action, in words and in blood. They have been defined and redefined, respected and protected by each generation of Americans.

It is these principles that have guided us at every juncture of the American journey and sustain every breath this nation takes. Think about it—our decisions to go to war, make peace, fight for civil rights, or go to the moon—each of these choices are in one way or another a manifestation and a defense of our values.

Many countries and organizations have beautifully written core values, but they are neither lived nor cemented into the collective consciousness of its people. They neither inform the decisions nor guide the visions. Instead they are mere beautiful words, in a national anthem or an inspiring plaque hung on a wall.

America lives the true meaning of its creeds—at least it tries to! And I believe that's what sustains our success. As a student of leadership, this is fascinating to me. The beauty, simplicity and elegance of the American story should be a model for healthy leadership—a values-centric leadership.

Family Values

So what are the best values? They are simply stated, clearly understood, and deeply believed and adhered to. They are principles that become part and parcel of our journey, woven into the consciousness of the people we lead. They whisk us away to the place of our dreams and protect us from ourselves, because they are grounded in truth.

Here is an example. As with any family, mine has had some successes and some failures. As I reflect on what our family values were (and still are), I see that even though my parents may not have had an academic understanding of "core values," they applied this very principle. I can trace every success we have had as a family to our core values.

My parents insisted on these principles. These were never written or plastered on the wall, but they were an ever-present theme in everything we did, spoke about, and practiced. These values were upheld by my parents without wavering. They made sure these values were followed, lived, and modeled.

1. Honor God.
2. Value education.
3. Love your family.
4. Work hard.
5. Aim high.

I remember one long night as a medical student, my mother came to my dorm room. I had to study all night for an important exam the next day, and I was struggling to stay awake. So she stayed up with me all night to encourage me

She honored education and hard work. Any time I faltered on sticking to these values, she showed up, gently, calmly, and resolutely insisting that there is no surrender and no retreat from these core principles. She upheld (and still upholds) the family values, even though she never calls them "family values."

Leadership Values

As a leader, what are the top five values that:

- Your life is built upon?
- Your team is built upon?
- Your family is built upon?

Allow your values to become guideposts, pointing you in the right direction as you embrace your purpose in life and leadership.

Growth

chapter 2

Chief Complaint

IT SEEMS LIKE I'M HITTING A WALL.

Prescription

BE INTENTIONAL ABOUT YOUR PERSONAL DEVELOPMENT.

Invest in Your Personal Growth

Healthy leadership is learned and developed in a daily and life-long pursuit of personal growth. Most of the time, it is immersive and aggressive experiences that cause us to break through to the next level. What experiences contribute most to developing strong leadership in you? Those in which you have to prove yourself. Experiences where you cannot rely or depend upon anyone else to make the tough calls and the crucial decisions of a leader. It's all on you. As I ponder how experience shapes our growth, I am reminded of my first week in residency.

It was my first night as an intern. I had just finished four years of intense learning in medical school. Anxious and scared, I reported to my post in the Emergency Room at John Peter Smith Hospital, the county hospital known for handling the worst cases in town.

The ER doctor quickly and casually introduced himself and told me that he would be taking care of the trauma patients on the one side of the ER, and that I needed to handle about 15 beds on the other side for the graveyard shift. I stood there in shock. *What?*

Is this guy crazy?

Me? By myself? These people have real emergencies, and I don't know what I am doing. This is my first night! But eager to prove myself, I was quick to tell him, "Yes sir, I will do my best." And he disappeared, never to be seen for the rest of the night.

Let me tell you, I had never been so scared as I was that night. But I had to perform. I could not leave. Luckily, the nurses who worked there were used to new interns like me. They knew that if something was really critical, they could go get the attending physician. But I didn't know that!

Simply put, I was baptized by fire that night.

I put my stethoscope around my neck and introduced myself to the nurses, who were not so impressed. All the ER beds were next to each other, with only curtains between them. So the groans, the shouts, and the smells mixed together to form an offensive atmosphere.

My first patient was a 17-year-old girl who had just tried to commit suicide by taking more than 20 sedative pills. I knew that could not be good, since it could cause her to stop breathing. I ordered charcoal to induce vomiting and looked at the nurse who was with me to make sure I was doing the right thing. He nodded his head in the affirmative.

The next patient was a 78-year-old Indian man who barely spoke English. He had not urinated for 2 days and was in severe pain, most likely from an enlarged prostate. I asked the nurse to put in a urinary catheter to drain the bladder. Two nurses tried unsuccessfully, and then proceeded to inform me that I needed to put it in myself. *What? That's really not good*, I thought. I had seen urinary catheters put in, but I had never put one in. Now I was being asked to do it in one of the most difficult cases. I hesitantly agreed. I tried…and tried…and tried. The poor man screamed and screamed. And everyone was watching me and listening.

The catheter never went in! *Now what?* All the trying had opened the urinary passage a little bit for him to have some urine come out to relieve the pain. I told him to wait for the urology team in the morning and hoped all would be okay.

Then there was the patient who had a foreign object in the eye, and the patient with a severe psychotic episode, screaming because she was seeing cockroaches everywhere, and the patient having the heart attack where I had to call the cardiologist at night and wake her up. Not a very pleasant call.

I had to perform.

People were depending on me. And I don't know how, but I did it! It was the most intense twelve hours of my life—and the most exhilarating! I became a doctor that night.

As I look back years later, I often wonder why they would do that to new doctors. I think it's because somehow they knew it was what it would take to make a good doctor. Teach them the stuff they need to know, then let them have intense experiences that test their knowledge, nerves and humanity.

And now I know that is what it takes to make a good leader. You must first be exposed to leadership principles. I could not have performed well that night if I had not gone through medical school. But then the crucial step to developing your leadership is intense and immersive experience. You have to make sure you have those as a leader.

Do not be afraid. Get in there and do it. Challenge yourself. There is nothing like performing under pressure to radically grow you as a doctor, a pastor, a firefighter, or a leader.

Don't Let Your Weaknesses Hijack Your Strengths

Your strengths are like the gas pedal of a car. Pressing the gas pedal will accelerate you forward. Similarly, the more we are living in and improving our strengths, the farther we will go in life.

But be careful! If growing and using your strengths is like pressing the gas pedal, your weaknesses are like having the emergency brake pulled while the car is trying to accelerate. No forward progress!

Improve strengths or weaknesses?

So what do we work on? Improving our strengths, or our weaknesses?

Many argue that the key to success is improving our strengths. They say that improving our strengths can take us from great to extraordinary, and that is where we can truly succeed. They argue that improving our weaknesses usually takes us only from bad to average—and that will not take us anywhere significant. And I agree. Working on our strengths will take us farther than improving upon our weaknesses. However, there seems to be a problem with this argument. It is apparent to most of us that people succeed because of their strengths, but they usually fail because certain weaknesses derail and sabotage those strengths.

One of my strengths is strategizing (that's my #1 strength from Tom Rath's *Strengths Finder 2.0*)[1]. One of my weaknesses is over-commitment. So when failure comes, it is not from being unable to strategize well, but from my lack of time to strategize because I am overcommitted.

Similarly, I see leaders who are great at project management, but they are terrible at caring for people and building relationships. Their success comes from finishing great projects, but that success is consistently derailed because of their weakness in relating to others.

So should I work on strategy or over-commitment? Should the leader above work on project management or relating to others?

The answer is *both*...and here is how to do it:

Consistently search for where you are strong and weak.

- **Character:** love, forgiveness, integrity, humility, discipline, attitude, etc.

- **Habits:** listening, organization, exercising, etc.

- **Personality traits:** creative, positive, thinker, doer, peaceful, analytical, etc.

- **Emotional abilities:** controlling anger and frustration, fear and courage, possessing the ability to know what others feel, etc.

- **Knowledge/Experience based skills:** in your leadership, business, parenting, communication, etc.

Daily discover and clarify your strengths.

- Begin to make a list of your strengths and define them. Literally write them down.

- The book *Strengths Finder 2.0* by Tom Rath[2] is a great tool to help you discover your strengths.

Aggressively work on those strengths and live in them!

- Read about them, attend seminars, talk to mentors/coaches.

- Be intentional to create a life journey that focuses on your strengths. For example, if one of your strengths is analyzing, become a strategy consultant. If you enjoy and are good at painting, become a painter.

Daily discover and clarify your weaknesses.

- Identify them, and write them down.

- Ask others whom you trust what they see as your weaknesses.

Dutifully identify which weaknesses stand in the way of your strengths.

- This is a KEY STEP: I believe all character issues, many habits, and many personal traits can potentially stand in the way of success. Many poor skills can as well. Determine what hinders your progress.

- As you prioritize what to work on, give the most emphasis to those areas that are most limiting to your strengths.

Aggressively work on those weaknesses and minimize them.

- If a weakness detracts from one of your strengths, attack it vigorously.

- In some cases it may even turn into a strength. In the least, work to remove it as a stumbling block.

I know so many leaders with amazing strengths. But these strengths have been *hijacked* by terrible weaknesses. This is true for most of us. We keep pressing the gas pedal, but go nowhere! With the emergency brake pulled, our efforts are futile. Know your strengths, grow your strengths, and live in them. Then, search and find the weaknesses that hijack your strengths, and relentlessly improve them.

Pay Attention in History Class

I hated history classes in school. I did not see the relevance. Remembering names, dates, and obscure events was intellectually annoying to my young mind.

But now, twenty years later, I love history! Not only for the pleasure and intrigue of discovering great stories, battles, and tragedies, but for the chance to unpack valuable lessons from humanity, society, and cultures. As a responsible citizen and student of leadership, I now want to learn everything I can about history.

So, how is history relevant to us?

I once heard an interview with Supreme Court Justice Anthony Scalia, who favors a more strict interpretation of the Constitution. He was asked why the Constitution should be venerated. He said that only a few times in the history of men, have learned persons of such a caliber as the writers of the Constitution come together to create such a magnificent document.

At first, I thought, "Really? Aren't we smarter *now* with our prestigious universities, abundance of immediate information, and so many people with PhD's, MD's, JD's?" But the reality is that, while we may not like to think about it, the engine for the human experience hasn't been upgraded for thousands of years. What we see by studying history is not unintelligent people trying to become advanced like we are. We see the human mind manifested, complete with its unbridled emotions, prejudices, perspectives, assumptions, and creativity. We see a picture of ourselves today and what we are capable of doing in the future.

While the narrative of our human story takes many twists and turns, the humanity of it remains the same. Our journey is directed by the human intellect, clothed by the human spirit, and subject to human error in thought and decision-making.

Consider the American story.

As an immigrant to the United States, I am fascinated by its history. It's a beautiful story of a people who in just over two centuries have built a nation based on three documents: the Declaration of Independence, the Constitution, and the Bill of Rights. And in relatively no time they became a world power—and a beacon of liberty and hope.

> *How did this happen? Who were the key people who brought us to this place? What were the pivotal points that propelled us forward and tipping points that sent us into crisis?*

As you aim to grow as a leader, don't neglect the study of history. Learn about our humanity, our heritage of leadership, and our history of successes and failures. What better way to seek wisdom than by reflecting on the journey of others.

Take Charge of Your Thoughts, Or They Will Take Charge of You

Are you in charge of your thoughts, or are they in charge of you? Are they automatic, reflexive and spontaneous? Or are they deliberate, controlled, and intentional? I discovered that if I want to manage my life well, I cannot let my brain dictate what I think about. This has given me tremendous freedom and control.

Do you ever find yourself obsessing about a thought, an idea or a problem? Do you wish you could stop thinking about it? You can! And you should acquire that skill.

Control Your Thoughts

The principle of controlling my thoughts was one of the biggest breakthroughs I ever had after years of personal defeat in one of the major challenges of my life: worry. A perfectionist by nature, I would obsess, fixate on, and become consumed by, a problem I had, a project I was in charge of, or a schedule I was trying to plan. I wouldn't be able to sleep well because I was thinking about it. I couldn't listen well, because I was thinking about it. I became a prisoner of that thought, at least until my brain decided that it had a satisfactory resolution.

I was aware that this was not a healthy way of thinking. It was exhausting, really. But still I wondered, *How can I stop my thoughts?* And, for that matter, *Why should I stop my thoughts? I always come up with solutions when I am thinking about the problem.*

Finally, I had a breakthrough! I discovered that worry can completely disappear if I can control my thoughts on the issues I am obsessing about.

Make Worry Disappear

- **Worry is solving problems at the wrong time.** Think about it. Worry is centered around something we perceive, correctly or not, as a problem. And when we worry, we are in essence trying to deal with it or solve it. The breakthrough for me was when I decided that it was okay—actually it was a must—not to solve problems all the time. Give your-self permission to have "problem-solving-free time." Decide when that is. If you solve problems all day at work, then when you come home, say after seven o'clock, give yourself permission not to solve problems.

- **Find out what thoughts are producing the worry.** Become cognizant of worry and anxiety. When you feel yourself entering that state, consciously ask yourself what you are thinking about in order to identify what triggers you to worry.

- **Aim to recognize them as soon as they happen.** Do it as quickly as possible, so you can take control of your thoughts, rather than letting your thoughts take charge of your whole day.

- **Start practicing the skill of controlling what you think about.** This is very hard, but it can be done! If I could teach you one thing in this whole book, it would be this. Here is the exercise that helped me attain this skill. Count to 50 or 100 without allowing any other thought to come to your mind, other than visualizing the written numbers. This takes a few weeks of dedicated practice. When you can do that, you will have conquered the hardest step in controlling your thoughts. Try it now.

Develop your thought life. Do not let your thoughts roam free. Take charge! Think about what you think about. For me it was worry. What is it for you? What thoughts pervade your mind that you wish you could stop?

Seek Opposing Opinions

I was fascinated with a recent interview with Senator George Mitchell. He was a Senator from Maine for fifteen years, Senate Majority Leader for six years, a special US envoy to Northern Ireland, credited for brokering peace between the UK and the IRA, a recent envoy to the Middle East, chairman of the Walt Disney Company, and the Chancellor of Queen's University in Belfast. I think we can safely say Senator Mitchell knows leadership.

As a preeminent diplomat and statesman, he has seen crisis first-hand and gotten to know leaders in peace, in war, and during bitter conflicts. For those reasons, when he speaks, many listen.

In the interview, he was asked, "What is the most disabling handicap leaders are susceptible to?" I remember perking up in my seat when he was asked that question. After hearing it, I hit the rewind button, and noted what he said:

> *The higher one goes in life, especially in government, the greater the capacity for self-delusion...meaning it is hard to get contradictory views and contradictory advice. You have to be aggressive in seeking it out. You have to search for contrary views.*

He went on to say...

One of the most amazing things is when you go around the world, and meet as many leaders of different countries as I have, to see how often they are misinformed, uninformed, and often delusional about the circumstances in which they find themselves. It is hard for leaders, and I mean it is especially hard for the President of the United States, to get a grip on reality. In other words, to get all the opposing views, to get a clear understanding to what's occurring because you live in a cocoon. You are surrounded by people who support what you say and don't contradict what you say. I believe a president must act aggressively to seek out contrary views.

If you read about leadership, this is not a new or revolutionary principle. But coming from such an astute personality, who has seen leaders from all over the world for over 30 years, makes it different to me!

The lessons I took away from Senator Mitchell are:

- Don't shun (in your heart) views that oppose yours. Listen to them wholeheartedly.

- If there do not seem to be opposing views to yours around you, seek them out aggressively.

- Work daily to quiet the story you tell yourself that, "what I know is true."

Senator Mitchell's advice starts and ends with wisdom and humility.

Embrace the "I Don't Know" Principle

Jeffery Immelt, the CEO of General Electric, was recently asked what he would consider to be the most important lesson he learned in the last ten years in that position.

Without hesitation Jeffrey answered,

> *I think it's humility and the curiosity that comes with it. In other words, the big mistakes you make are when you stop asking questions. But if you're hungry and humble, you are always digging for that extra piece of knowledge...*

While it is somewhat fashionable for CEO's and thought leaders to list humility in leadership as one of the most desired qualities, I believe we should all apply it practically in our lives. Here is how I understand it:

I call it the "I Don't Know" principle.

A successful leader should seek to balance the "I know"—confidence in yourself, your team, and your vision—with the "I don't know." The "I don't know" principle, or humility, says this:

1. I could be wrong.
2. What I know is not from me.
3. Where I have arrived is not because of me.

4. I have been given so I can give.
5. I am not better than any other human being.
6. I am not invincible.
7. We are all stupid, but in different things.

I recently interviewed several executives, including a CEO of a hospital, for the job of running my clinics. I was astounded that some were firmly in the "I know" zone. But it also seemed clear to me that the more successful a leader was that I interviewed, the more humility I sensed.

Remember, you don't know it all. Take ownership of the "I Don't Know" principle because that's when you will truly empower others to come alongside you, to strengthen and add value to you, the team, and the vision. Questioning what you know and what you believe is a catalyst for personal growth. Aim to always be the student. Always be the one taking notes, the one doing the listening, calmly reflecting and learning. Intentionally challenge yourself to learn all you can learn and to be all you can be, while humbly embracing the "I Don't Know" principle.

Vision

chapter 3

Chief Complaint

I THINK I AM STUCK IN A RUT.

Prescription

ENLARGE YOUR VISION.

Think Big, Act Bold

I encourage you to put timidity and fear aside and ask yourself two questions about your life, plans, and vision.

1. Am I thinking big?
2. Am I acting bold?

Ask these questions often. And when you find that you are not, change your course.

Years ago, I met author and speaker Dr. Tony Baron at a conference. After we chatted for a while he gave me a copy of his latest book, *The Art of Servant Leadership*[3], and personalized the book with the following note:

To my friend Wes,
Here's to thinking big and acting bold as a servant leader,
Mark 10:45, Tony Baron

These simple words resonated with me then—and to this day I refer to them when I need to refocus and strengthen my resolve.

I don't know about you, but my instinct is not to think big, but to think safe and small. My inclination is not to act bold, but to act with timidity and hesitation. And my tendency is not to serve others, but to serve myself. As leaders, we must reject these natural instincts. Rather let us commit to this:

I resolve that in whatever I do, I will think big, act bold, and serve others!

Think Big

Five signs to know if your thinking is big:

1. It inspires you and inspires others.
2. It scares you and scares others.
3. Many people around you, even the ones close to you, think you are crazy.
4. Failure may mean real pain and loss.
5. It invigorates you and lights a fire in your belly.

Thinking big starts with dedicating time to think intentionally. While thinking big is not fantasy thinking (for example, creating a time machine and being transported to the 3rd century BC may be simply impossible), big thinking and fantasy thinking are close cousins. So get comfortable with thinking outside the box.

Act Bold

Five signs to know if you are acting boldly:

1. You regularly act on your big thoughts.
2. You act even if you are not 100% sure.
3. You always try something new.
4. You forge ahead regardless of howling winds of rejection, criticism, and failure.
5. You act when you have a gut instinct.

Remember that acting boldly does not mean acting at the wrong time—be patient and wait for God's timing. It does not mean acting in the wrong manner—don't be reckless. And it does not mean acting in a hurtful way to others—don't be hurtful.

Beware of Dream Killers

The biggest killers of big thinking and bold action are small-thinking people and those who are afraid to fail. People around me can either kill or build my big thinking and bold action. People I love, those whom I truly listen to, have an astounding impact on my thinking and action. So, be clear as to the gifts of the people around you. Here is how I fill my inner-circle:

1. **The Encouragers**: Whatever you do, they believe in you. These people fill your bucket.

2. **The Big Thinkers**: When you share a big dream with them, they tell you that you should think bigger. They help you enlarge your thinking and dreams.

3. **The Correctors**: They immediately jump to find the errors in your thinking, and they are good at it.

4. **The Realists**: They bring you back to reality and help you focus on what *is*, not on what *can be*.

Identify who has which gift. We naturally want the correctors' and realists' approval. But do not go to them first. They will kill your dream and your big thoughts. They have a role, but not at the beginning of your dream. So as you move forward, spend some time and assess these key people in your life.

Serve Others

Dr. Baron ended his brief inscription in my book with Mark 10:45, which reads, "For even the Son of Man did not come to be served, but to serve, and to give his life as a ransom for many." If you value the impact of effective leadership, and if you honor Jesus as a perfect Leader, this verse should be a guidepost for you.

Most leaders are asking, "What can you do for me?" Servant leaders ask genuinely, "What can I do for you?" When was the last time you asked your people that question, and were willing to act upon their responses?

So I dare you to start thinking big, acting bold, and serving others.

Take Risks

Our capacity for taking risks is often what sets us apart in leadership, as in life. Here are the normal stages that we need to guard against:

1. You risk, try, and fight as you scale the mountains of great dreams.
2. You make gains.
3. Your focus shifts to maintaining your gains.
4. You stop risking, and you stop punching through the walls of the impossible.
5. You start fading and declining.

You see this clearly in businesses and corporations. When they start, they are aggressive. They take risks with their capital, proposing bold ideas and making gutsy initiatives. That is, until they succeed. Then, they stop. They become afraid to lose what they've gained. They go into a phase of just trying to protect their gains. Risk-taking ends. No more daring. No more boldness or courage.

Whether it's your organization, your team or your life—relaxing and not taking risks usually means declining. When we become comfortable as the caretakers of our gains, it is in that very moment that our decline begins.

So, where are you now in your life? What options are before you? Which one is the safest, and which one raises your blood pressure and heart rate a little? If your life is going to be full of passion and effectiveness, never stop taking risks and pushing yourself outside of your comfort zone. Dare to do the impossible and reach for the improbable! Dare to fulfill your purpose.

Be the risk-taker of your life, not the caretaker of your gains.

Just Jump

Leadership requires courage. Many times in our leadership journey, we are faced with situations that require us to make a tough judgment call and take action. While we must do everything we can to prepare, gather information, talk to people, and take the pulse of the team, it all often leads to one moment of truth. People are counting on us to make a decision. And, ready or not, sometimes we have to just jump.

Some time ago, my cousin Andrew, who had gone skydiving several times, said that I should do it, too. Not long after that, some of my co-workers at the hospital also challenged me to try it. I responded with an emphatic "NO!" So soon afterward, while I was performing a colonoscopy, one of the nurses darted into the operating room and tauntingly said, "Chicken!"

I reserved my spot that day.

I Googled how to write a will.

Hours before I was to leave for the jump, my brother Roger called me. The call was short and sweet. He asked, "Do you have your will written?" After a pause and a smile, I replied, "I think that's a good idea." So I spent twenty minutes Googling "how to write a will in Texas." It was not easy to write it. But I did.

A few weeks prior, I Googled "skydiving." But "skydiving fatalities" popped up first. I clicked on the first article. It was about a 49-year-old New York executive who decided to jump tandem for his 50th birthday. With a big group of people watching him, he plunged to his death. After reading that, I figured the will was a good idea after all.

Then I took a shower…you know that advice mom gives about clean underwear! (Although as an intern, when I had to rip the clothes off of trauma patients, I never recall anyone checking underwear!) But a few people who are very close to me were going to be there, including my mom and nieces. Yes, I repressed the thoughts. After all, the fatality rate for tandem jumps is only one in three million. But I couldn't help thinking, *It would not be a good sight for them to see!*

As if the jump was not scary enough, I then began to contemplate the landing. Just weeks before, I treated a 27-year-old patient who, during his service in the 101st Airborne, had broken his ankle and hip while landing. Of course, he was jumping from 800 feet behind enemy lines. We would be jumping from 10,000 feet.

All this preparation was leading up to my moment of truth—the jump.

What the heck am I doing?

As the plane was making its way higher into the air, being the thinker that I am, I considered how what I was about to do was similar to other things I am scared to do in my life. It is common in life and leadership to be faced with conquering fear as we move ourselves and our teams forward. And I found myself thinking about how in those situations as well, I needed to *just jump!*

At 10,000 feet the plane door opened. And I was elected by the nurses, who had come along, to be the first to take the plunge. They wanted to see the scared look on my face. (And the video that was taken clearly showed it.)

The cold air rushed in. We start crawling to the door. And I was thinking to myself, *What the heck am I doing?* We sat at the edge of the plane with my feet dangling in the air outside. We rocked back. Seconds seemed like eternity.

We jumped.

And a split second after that, a photo was snapped. I don't have a conscious memory of that moment. So if it were not for the photo, I would not be aware of it. In the photo, my eyes are closed. I don't remember closing them. I guess my neuronal pathways were overloaded and my blood oxygen low due to the high altitude.

The trip to the ground was exhilarating, jarring, and psychologically intense—like nothing else I had ever done. I survived. The will I wrote would not be executed that day.

Will you do it?

Jumping from the plane reminded me of another jump I made twelve years ago. As a medical student, I would go with two of my friends, Allen and Jim, to the school's outdoor pool in the dead of winter. We would jump into the frigid water and swim a few laps.

That moment right before the jump—whether out of an airplane, into freezing water, or into the scariest places you and I dare to tread in our own lives—at that pivotal moment, a mental voice jeers at us, *Will you do it?* It's a moment when we find ourselves either shrinking back or conquering fear.

That split second after we jump, we usually don't remember much. We are overloaded with anxiety and panic. But we do remember a few seconds and minutes after that…a few hours, days, and years. And we remember and celebrate the rare courage we exhibited in that moment before we jumped.

If we are to grow and progress as leaders, we must be willing to put ourselves out there, right at the edge of a 10,000 foot drop with our feet dangling in the air. Whether we feel prepared or not, whether we feel scared or not, whether we feel skilled or not—we must face the moments where all that is left for us, is to *just jump.*

Productivity

chapter 4

Chief Complaint

I DON'T HAVE ENOUGH MINUTES IN MY DAY.

Prescription

FOCUS ON INCREASING YOUR PRODUCTIVITY, NOT YOUR TIME.

Change Your Life
30 Seconds at a Time

I came upon a simple little time management trick that allows me to do the things I really want to do (and really need to do), but always seem to put off until later.

Regardless of how successful, accomplished, disciplined, or focused we are, there are always a handful of actions that we dread doing—and usually don't do, even though we are capable. Sometimes, avoiding these actions limits our progress in life and in leadership.

It could be figuring our taxes, organizing our office, writing an important letter, or drafting our company's strategic plan. You know, those tasks that we end up doing at the very last minute—only to avoid major disaster. These few items are also a source of pain. They taunt us, saying, *You are not disciplined enough to take care of this.*

Can you think of anything right now that you wish you could get yourself to do? Here is a simple but powerful time-management technique that helps me overcome this annoying human tendency.

Here Is What You Do

1. Get out your stopwatch. (I use the one on my iPhone.)

2. Tell yourself, *I will make myself do this task that I am dreading for only 30 seconds.* The deal you are making with yourself is that after 30 seconds you can abort and stop doing the task at hand.

3. Start the action that you are dreading and putting off.

4. Most of the time, after 30 seconds of doing it, your discomfort and hesitation are decreased significantly—often enough to finish the job!

I use this technique several times per week. I use it for mundane tasks and sometimes even for important ones.

In the study of chemistry we learn about "activation energy." This is the rate-limiting step for a chemical reaction to actually take place. Chemists use different types of techniques and agents (called *catalysts)* to get a chemical reaction to move beyond that limit. It is downhill from there. The technique I've just given is designed to get you over the hump in just 30 seconds.

After all, you can do anything for 30 seconds. And often that's just the catalyst we need to get us moving.

Understand the Power of Good and Bad Habits

Habits are imprinted on our brains almost like tattoos on the skin. We can make new ones, but it is a grueling process to remove the old ones. I learned a lot about the influence habits have on our lives from Charles Duhigg's book, *The Power of Habit: Why We Do What We Do in Life and Business.*[4] And it's made a difference in how I think about the good and bad habits in my life as a leader. Understanding these principles can be very helpful on your journey to becoming a more productive leader.

The Anatomy of a Habit

When you do something so many times that you don't think about it anymore (or very minimally), that is a habit. Habits are routines that we do with tremendous ease, almost robotically, or automatically. These routines can be simple or complex.

When driving, if you want to signal a left turn, you don't think about reaching with your left hand and pushing the lever. You do it automatically. Similarly, a surgeon does not think much when he hits a small blood vessel that starts bleeding. He calls for "cautery," and zaps it quickly to stop the bleeding.

A habit is formed by repeating a sequence of events many times until it becomes automatic. We take this ability for granted. If you think about it, however, this is a mind-blowing ability our brain has. I can in essence teach my brain almost anything, regardless of how complex, and it will do it with ease and fluidity and at a moment's notice. The only thing I have to do is repeat that action enough times.

Habits can be broken into three basic parts:

- **Cue**—a trigger for us to start. (example: the thought that we need to make a left turn)

- **Routine**—the sequence of events of which the habit consists. (example: reaching with our left hand and pushing the signal lever down)

- **Reward**—the good feeling we get from finishing the routine. (example: feeling good that we followed the law and signaled correctly)

What is most interesting is that our brains dedicate a special place to the storage of habits. These procedural, automatic processes we follow are stored in a specific part of our brains called the basal ganglia. This is different from the location where the information needed to perform the task is stored. Only the sequence is stored in the basal ganglia.

Let me illustrate. A patient who has a stroke in which brain cells die in the area that stores information about where he lives, will not be able to describe to you where his house is, tell you his address, or give you directions. However, if you place him at the entrance of his neighborhood, he can walk to his house. That is because his basal ganglia (assuming the stroke has not affected that area as well) contains separate information that is related to the sequence and mechanics of an action (in this example, going left or right on the streets of his neighborhood).

Why is this applicable and important? Because our brains maintain a special capacity to learn new habits and routines. To use a computer analogy, we have a dedicated hard drive for habit formation. We should use it!

How Habits Become Automatic

This ease of performing simple or complex actions can make or break us as individuals and as leaders at home and at work. When you form good habits, you do good things with ease. When you form bad habits, you do bad things with ease. If you keep habits that set you up for success, then you perform successful actions with ease.

Most of us are not conscious of forming new good habits. Most are also not aware that almost everything we do is in some way a habit. "We are creatures of habit," is not just a cliché. It is the truth. What we think of and do is largely preprogrammed.

Even our emotions are also habitually controlled. If we want growth, progress, and freedom, we need to understand the power of our habits.

For a habit to be created, systematic steps have to be performed the same way. Let me give you an example.

As a family doctor, I have seen thousands of patients for the symptoms of a cough and sore throat. I always do the same things. I ask the patient to sit on the exam table and tell him to, "Say, 'Ahhhh.'" Then I feel his neck lymph nodes and look into his ears. I have done this so many times that it is automatic. If something changes, like let's say the patient does not sit on the examination table, then I am not as efficient, because I am not using the automatic pathways from my basal ganglia. I have to think more, so it is a much slower process.

An experiment[5] was done where a small mouse was placed in a T-shaped container with cheese on the left end of the top of the T. Measuring its brain's electrical impulses, the first few times the mouse was searching for the cheese, it had high brain activity because it was thinking. After 20 times, the brain activity became low. The mouse found the cheese quickly and easily. Then, when the cheese was moved to the other side of the T, the mouse had high brain activity again—it struggled to find the cheese because it had to start thinking again. But again after many times, finding the cheese became easy for it.

Creating Good Habits

- **Understand the power of habits.** We should understand that habit formation can make very complex or difficult activities simple and easy. Of course, this only occurs after conscious effort and many repetitions. Our habits determine our successes and failures.

- **Be intentional about forming good habits.** How? Design a routine for something you want to do, be very conscious in the beginning, and "force" yourself until it becomes automatic. Much research has recently been discussed as to how many days it takes to form a new habit. But I really think the results of this research are irrelevant. Here's how to form a new habit: keep doing it until it becomes easy and automatic, regardless of how long it may take.

- **Focus on forming new habits to replace your bad habits.** For example, you become aware that you have the habit of gossiping. So you design a new habit of doing the following: When you hear something bad about a person, you will say something *good* about that person to someone else. Now of course, at first this is very unnatural and hard. But like any other routine, after repetition it will become automatic.

Eliminating Bad Habits

- **Habits cannot be erased.** Remember that you are always in danger of slipping into an old habit because it is forever imprinted on your basal ganglia. However, with repeated practice of a new habit, you can become less likely to respond to the old cue in the same way.

- **Move the cheese.**[6] One way to alter a habit is to change the routine. When a patient who would like to quit smoking visits my clinic, I ask them about the routine they take that triggers their desire to smoke. If being at a certain restaurant makes them want to smoke (cue), then we discuss the possibility of not going to that restaurant. This takes careful analysis of your bad habits. If you are able to alter any of the steps of a bad habit, your brain cannot execute it automatically anymore.

- **Know that your bad behaviors are usually nothing but habits.** Going back to gossiping: when you hear something bad about another person (cue), you find the next person you see in your office and tell them all about it (routine), and then you feel good that you told someone (reward). Most of us have done this before. It becomes an automatic response.

What do we do with our bad habits? How can they be eliminated? If we knew the answer to this, we would not have an epidemic of smoking or overeating. Like tattoos, they cannot be erased, not easily anyway. However, there are some things that can be done. Become aware of the cues, routines, and rewards and have a plan. Either remove the cues, change the routine, or remove the reward. Awareness is key. You can change your life by changing your habits. Start working on them today!

Make Sure Your People Are Productive

When I see a leader perpetually fixated on his tasks—focused in like a laser beam on his work—I know he is probably not the most productive and effective he can be as a leader. If for hours he is sitting at his desk, looking at his computer, and making "important" phone calls, he may believe he is doing the work of a leader. But I can tell that this person has never made the transition from a non-leader to a leader, because a leader's most important work is with his *people*, not with his *tasks*.

Dividing Time

When we are not in a leadership position, we are most productive when we are hard at work accomplishing our duties. Our time may be spent like this:

15% of our time is dedicated to thinking, strategizing, and dreaming

85% of our time is dedicated to getting things done

Many times when we move into a leadership position, we tend to continue the same pattern of focus.

As productive leaders, however, we should our spend time more like this:

40% of our time is dedicated to thinking, strategizing, and dreaming

20% of our time is dedicated to getting things done

40% of our time is dedicated to empowering others and removing obstacles to allow our team members to be productive

Wasting Time vs. Spending Time

When I talk to some leaders, they often complain about how much time they have to "waste" by talking, resolving issues, clarifying, or empowering. And I think to myself (and sometimes tell them), "That is exactly what the work of a leader is." *The job of a productive leader is to make sure others are productive.* Period. To deal with the issues at hand that may be impeding their effectiveness. Not to tolerate immature behavior, gossip, or drama, but rather to navigate the normal human challenges that naturally come up.

I recently went to dinner with a business associate. It was a great time for fellowship and to connect. Having a very full schedule, I naturally would have preferred to stay home, read a book, write, or go have yogurt with my nephew or niece. But then I reminded myself…this *is* the work of a leader. I needed that time to connect with that person, to hear his concerns from the heart.

Leading people can be messy and unpredictable. When the "people work" gets too stressful, demanding, or physically and emotionally exhausting, I have to remind myself: This *is* the work of a leader. As leaders, we have more than a job to do; we have people to lead. If all we want to do is the task at hand and we are not willing to work with people consistently, then we should consider resigning from a position of leadership.

Focus on What (Not How)

Don't limit your dreams to things you know how to achieve. The *how* will reveal itself when you can clearly answer, "*What* do I want get to?" The clearer you see the *what*, the faster the *how* will come.

I recently listened to an interview with Arnold Schwarzenegger. He was asked how he was able to go from being a kid born into a poor family in Austria, growing up without electricity or running water, to becoming a bodybuilding legend, a mega movie star and a two-term governor of California. Arnold quickly shared the answer. He said:

> *I always had the most extraordinary talent for visualizing. I always as a kid had the vision, and the vision was so real that I really felt that I could accomplish and turn those visions into reality.*

He did not know exactly *how* to get there, but he knew exactly *what* he wanted to get to.

On May 25th, 1961, President John F. Kennedy, speaking to a special joint session of Congress, challenged the nation to go to the moon. At the time only 50% of NASA scientists thought it was even possible. He defined the *what*, and somehow the nation was galvanized to discover the *how*. On July 21st, 1969, we landed on the moon!

My mentor, Rev. Peter Rahme, once told me, "When you dream, dream big!" Don't worry about how to get there for now. Yes, there will be a time to answer the *how* and to form the strategy, but not just yet. Not until you answer the *what*—and it must be a *what* that inspires you, compels you, and drives you forward with passion.

I recently met with the CEO of very large and successful hospital. I asked him to give me some leadership advice. He told me, "In my position, it is not my role to figure out the *how*. But it is my role to figure out the *where* and *why*."

Successful leaders never limit their destinations by their limitations. They keep their focus on their target, which is their *what* or *where*. And they partner together with their teams to strategize (determine *how*), overcome obstacles, and move forward to accomplish their goals.

Create a Strategy

War is a time when leadership is crucial. It is a time when lives are at stake. But even in ordinary life, I also believe that leadership absolutely matters. While people may not die because of our failure to lead well, many will undoubtedly suffer. Below are "The Nine Principles of War" from the *US Army Field Manual*[7] and a few of my thoughts on each one. These are key principles that, when applied, make our leadership more effective.

The Nine Principles of War

While most of these principles seem simple to understand, they are not always simple to apply. So, what can we learn from leadership in the military?

1. **Objective**—Direct all efforts to a clearly defined, decisive, and obtainable goal.

   - What is your objective?

   - Is it clear?

2. **Offensive**—Seize the initiative in a decisive manner.

   - Some teams play to win, and some play not to lose. Have the courage to pounce on what you are trying to accomplish. We need to simply "bring home the bacon!"

   - If you always wait for the perfect moment to act, you never will.

3. **Mass**—Concentrate your combat power at a time when it matters most.

   - Use and concentrate your greatest strengths. Do you know what they are?

   - Use them at the right time to achieve your objective.

4. **The Economy of Force**—Allocate minimum essential combat power to secondary efforts.

   - You cannot be everything to all people.

   - Know what is secondary and give it your minimum effort.

5. **Maneuver**—Place the enemy in a position of disadvantage through the flexible application of combat power.

   - Be flexible, adaptable, and ready to change with the demands on the ground.

   - Draw great plans, but be ready to change them during battle.

6. **Unity of Command**—All forces shall be under one responsible commander with authority to direct all forces in pursuit of a unified purpose.

   - Take the responsibility as a leader.

   - Delegate authority and responsibility, but be accountable to the final result yourself.

7. **Security**—Never permit the enemy to acquire an unexpected advantage.

    - Obtain knowledge and understanding of competitors' strategies, tactics, doctrines, and staff.

    - Understand clearly what you are up against and what the risks are to your team or organization.

8. **Surprise**—Strike the enemy at a time or place or in a manner for which he is unprepared.

    - Choose the right time to launch your objective.

    - Use the element of surprise to your advantage.

9. **Simplicity**—Simple plans and concise orders minimize misunderstanding and confusion.

    - Communicate clearly.

    - Simplicity is crucial for success.

I was honored recently to attend the change of command for the US Army's 95th Division at Fort Sill in Lawton, Oklahoma. What struck me was how even a great military general's influence is not based on force, but on honor. It reminded me that great leadership is simply *great leadership*. Whether in a father at home, a pastor at church, a boss at work, a mayor in a city, or a general on the battlefield—in its essence, leadership differs very little. Great leadership is about depth of character, wisdom of approach, and a magnetic vision. And great leadership requires: Guts. Service. Sacrifice.

Connection

chapter 5

Chief Complaint

I CAN'T GET EVERYONE TO SUPPORT
MY VISION.

Prescription

LEARN HOW TO CONNECT WITH PEOPLE.

See People, Not Employees

How are you relating to your people? Do you see those you lead as workers and employees, or as people? People with pains, worries and fears. People with strengths, hopes and dreams. People who hurt, love and cry.

Have you ever worked for someone who was only interested in what you did, but not really in you? I have, more than once. And those leaders were consistently ineffective with me and others.

Meeting People's Needs

Tony Schwartz, president and CEO of The Energy Project and the author of *Be Excellent at Anything*, thinks outside the office when it comes to employee schedules and work locations. In an article for the Harvard Business Review[8], Schwartz explains that the best way to cultivate productive employees is to treat them like adults.

One of the senior members of his team works from home three days a week in order to have more time with her school-age children and to avoid a three-hour commute. Another works from home the first day she returns from a business trip. And he even granted a married couple on his team permission to work out of the country simply because they wanted to experience another culture. He reports that it works "seamlessly" and that every one of them is highly productive.

In fact, no one has left the company in over a decade. Schwartz says it all boils down to trust and treating people like adults. He says, "The better you meet people's needs, the better they'll meet yours."

Seeing Others as People First

Why is it important to see people, not employees?

1. **Simply, it is the right thing to do.** We all need to be respected, listened to and loved. We all want our lives to mean something worthwhile. We all long to be a part of something great. We all want to be happy. As leaders, we should consider it our responsibility to care for the people we lead. Take it seriously. Impact their lives positively.

2. **Your culture will become people-oriented.** When you demonstrate humanity to those you lead, they will demonstrate humanity back to you. And trust me, you will need it. My staff recently gave me a card. Each of them had written in it words of appreciation. I knew they meant it. And it meant a lot to me. See, I tell them all the time how I love them. Because I do. I see them as family. And that's how I want them to see me. And more importantly, that's how I want them to see each other.

3. **We will become truly effective with others.** When you see people as people, they will allow you unprecedented access into their lives and hearts. They will follow you and care about you and your vision because you care about them and their vision.

But remember that we should never care because of what we may get in return. We should care just because we should care.

I know it is hard to see the person sometimes. We may be overwhelmed, overworked and overstretched. But, let us stop this crazy rush, truly see people, and dare to care.

Resist the Temptation to Keep People at Arm's Length

If you hesitate to build relationships with those you lead, you are not alone. There is an entire school of thought that supports keeping yourself at a distance from those you lead. However, healthy leadership is built on healthy relationships. And relationships cannot be built from a distance.

We need to invest in relationships that can withstand the howling winds of misunderstanding and change, lasting for a lifetime. Relationships that pierce through to the core, and hang on for dear life through the trying times of progress. Relationships that have depth and breadth, rooted in love and sacrifice, built with care and intentionality, and cemented with commitment and loyalty.

We need to commit to building relationships that are forged in inspiring journeys and fulfilling destinies—relationships that breathe respect and openness, always finding commonality and searching for ways to connect and understand in even deeper ways. Why don't we? Why do so many leaders hesitate to build strong relationships?

Six Reasons Leaders Hesitate to Build Relationships

1. It is hard. Building relationships takes work. It takes consistency and sacrifice. As a leader, I am often tired and overworked, and quite honestly I have little emotional energy at times to put in what it takes to build strong relationships. The fact is, if we prefer to do only what is easy, then we are simply not ready to lead on the big stage. As leaders, we should be willing to pay whatever price necessary to have the strongest and deepest relationships possible.

2. We think it is a waste of time. Some think that leadership is just about getting things done, and the fuzzy stuff about relationships is simply a waste of time. If you are a task-oriented person, you are likely to feel that way. However, I can assure you that getting things done will not be as efficient if the relationships are poor. Maintaining a relationship may take you away from doing tasks, however you will produce much more in the end when you have strong relationships with others on your team.

3. We simply don't have time. You may value building relationships, however you may feel you have no time. If we don't have time to have strong relationships with those we lead, we should simply get out of leadership...because we will not be effective. When we acknowledge that relationships are part and parcel of successful leadership, we will start budgeting the time for them.

4. We think we should not because they will "run all over us." I have previously felt disrespected by those I befriended when I was in leadership. So I thought at the time that the problem was the friendship, and that I should stay cold, serious, and distant. Then I discovered that this was not true. The problem was never the friendship or the close relationship, and this was an immature understanding of leadership. The problem was the unclear boundaries. I discovered that any healthy human relationship should have boundaries. However, for boundaries to work in a close relationship, they have to be stated clearly, kindly, firmly, and as early as possible. We also have to be consistent with reminding others of them. This takes emotional maturity, experience, and courage.

5. We think we would not be able to "get rid of" that person. Dr. Henry Cloud wrote a book called *Necessary Endings*[9] that addresses this topic. Yes, if you are close to someone, it is hard to end the relationship. However if we are to succeed in leadership, we simply must learn when to and how to end a relationship, and more importantly how to process it mentally and emotionally. This is not easy. But if we don't master this, we will end up with mediocre teams because we are unable to end the relationships that should end, and become afraid to form close relationships with those we lead.

6. We don't know how to build relationships successfully. You may shy away from building relationships because you think you are not good at it. You may be right! Remember that competence precedes confidence. So, let's get competent in this extremely important area of leadership, and then we will build the confidence to practice great relationship building.

If you desire people to genuinely support you and your vision, you must connect with them and foster a relationship. You must move past traditionally professional, distant and sterile relationships with those you work with—keeping people at an arm's length. Rather, nurture professional relationships that are personal, warm, and caring.

Know How Your People Feel

Good leaders know what their people *do*. Exceptional leaders know how their people *feel*.

Your people's feelings matter.

Do you monitor the emotional pulse of your team? It is a vital sign in your leadership that cannot be ignored. And just like in our human bodies, having a healthy pulse matters *all the time*. It must be monitored even more closely when stressors are present on your team: for instance, when change is taking place, when you are proposing a new vision, or simply when you are forging ahead as a team.

Why does it matter? Because you cannot effectively lead people if you don't know them and care about them. You should be able to affect how they feel about you, the team, the vision or the organization because you have invested into your relationship with them. Great generals and coaches know this. They know that when their armies or teams feel discouraged or disempowered, success will be difficult to achieve and maintain.

Monitor how your people feel.

In gastrointestinal endoscopy, as a heavily sedated patient's stomach and intestines are being examined, vital signs are closely monitored. High tech machines are used and always beep at a certain speed indicating the patient's heart rate, and at a certain pitch indicating their oxygen level. This machine is always on. If there is any deviation in their vital signs the medical team will know immediately. Similarly, great leaders constantly monitor their people's feelings and their teams' morale, and not just at the beginning of a project, or when there are problems.

I meet daily with my team, and I usually come in with a list of issues that we need to discuss. But more importantly, when I arrive for the day, I greet everyone personally. And I have one thing on my mind: How does each of them feel today? This will tell me how much I can push or introduce change, and who I need to back off of. By knowing how people feel, I eliminate unnecessary problems.

Whether you are a president of a country, a pastor of a church, a manager in a factory, or the CEO of a company, know how your people feel. If your people feel like a million bucks as a part of your team…success will follow.

Accept that People Will Hurt You; Keep Them Close Anyway

Sometimes you invest in people for a long time—you love them, nurture them, and give them opportunities—the best way you know how. Then they leave you or hurt you, or don't rise up to your expectations. Maybe they simply fail you or even betray you. Getting close to people when you are in leadership can be risky.

A few years ago a very trusted employee, to whom we had given much opportunity and care, abruptly left the company. Not only that, she started recruiting others from our team to go with her. We felt betrayed and honestly, hurt.

As leaders, shouldn't we keep people at a distance?

Our first instinct was to stop investing in people and to keep them at a distance. Isn't that the old leadership advice we've all heard at some point: "Avoid getting close to people when you are in leadership. Keep yourself at a distance."

For a long time, I was not sure how to handle these situations emotionally until I heard a very simple, yet powerful, principle taught by John Maxwell. This was a tipping point for me in my leadership. It is a principle I remind myself and others of often. He said, "If you hold people at a distance, they can't hurt you. But if you hold them at a distance, they can't help you."

As I look back at the last few years of my leadership journey, since I started trying to apply this principle, I've been hurt by a handful of people. But I would not avoid that hurt in a million years if it meant that I'd have to give up the wonderful relationships of trust and camaraderie that have also come because I was willing to risk being wounded. No matter how good you become at discerning people's intent and character, you cannot be 100% immune to being hurt by others. But that doesn't mean we shut people out and keep them at a distance. Ideally, we challenge ourselves to mature to such a place that we can accept that people may hurt us, but we choose to take the risk, and extend forgiveness and compassion when it's required.

Keep people close to you.

So I challenge you to do the following the next time you get hurt—you know, that kind of hurt where you feel let down or insulted—that hurt where you feel like you've been punched in the stomach. Say to yourself, *I will not stop loving people and bringing them close to me, regardless of the cost or the hurt.* Of course, you may have to place a boundary with that specific person. But don't do it with everyone as a result of your hurt.

Even though relationships are where pain occurs, that's also where healing occurs. Even though that's where anguish and agony may happen, that's also where growth, beauty, and the mystery of God's love are manifested. When you get hurt, hold on to your heart for a moment, but only for a moment. Then open it back up to the world because that's where a leader's heart belongs.

Endeavor to Live "Beyond Forgiveness"

The need for forgiveness presupposes that someone hurt or offended you, and they need your forgiveness and grace. And this happens when we become close to people. But what if we challenged ourselves not to get hurt or offended in the first place? We could move past the all-consuming cycle of "being hurt, then forgive" to the place of living "beyond forgiveness." This is where mature leaders live.

A Mother's Perspective

This is a very important topic for all of us as leaders. The best illustration I can give that we can all relate to is how a mother rarely needs to forgive her children. When children misbehave or act outwardly offensive to her, it seems that for the most part a mother's thinking is:

My child is acting this way because:

- He is stressed.
- I was not able to coach him better.
- He is tired.

It is never "because he is a bad person." Mothers think of their children as eternally good, and reason that they do bad things because they cannot help it or because they don't know better.

This kernel of truth has the power to release you from the bondage of hurt and hate. Seeing everyone as good, but occasionally doing bad things because they are weak or don't know better, has completely revolutionized my life.

Writing Your Hurts in the Sand

We should all consider adopting the sentiment offered in this inspirational story[10] of forgiveness:

> *A story tells that two friends were walking through the desert. During some point of the journey they had an argument, and one friend slapped the other one in the face. The one who got slapped was hurt, but without saying anything, wrote in the sand:*
>
> *TODAY MY BEST FRIEND SLAPPED ME IN THE FACE.*
>
> *They kept on walking until they found an oasis, where they decided to take a bath. The one who had been slapped got stuck in the mire and started drowning, but the friend saved him. After he recovered from the near drowning, he wrote on a stone:*
>
> *TODAY MY BEST FRIEND SAVED MY LIFE.*
>
> *The friend who had slapped and saved his best friend asked him, "After I hurt you, you wrote in the sand. And now, you write on a stone. Why?" The other friend replied,*

"When someone hurts us we should write it down in sand where the winds of forgiveness can erase it away. But, when someone does something good for us, we must engrave it in stone where no wind can ever erase it."

LEARN TO WRITE YOUR HURTS IN THE SAND AND TO CARVE YOUR BENEFITS IN STONE.

This principle is immensely applicable to us as leaders. As we lead people, our actions toward them will mirror how we feel about them. Just like a mother, or a best friend, we can show them that we believe they are ultimately good people, who just make mistakes. We demonstrate that we expect them to be human and accept them for who they are. And in so doing, we remove the pressure to perform and simply empower them to be themselves. We communicate that we believe in them. We create a culture that rejects drama and back-biting, and encourages compassion and acceptance.

Living in the "Beyond Forgiveness" Zone

As I have come to this point in my own growth journey, I have accumulated a few commitments to help me stay focused on staying in the "beyond forgiveness" zone and away from the "hurt-forgive" cycle. This takes continual work and reminding. To that end, I read these principles below on a regular basis. I want to share them with you because they help me keep my heart in the right place. I hope they will help you as well.

As you read the following lines, think of a person who has hurt you, and think about the people you lead.

I will never make you feel small.
I will celebrate the breath of the Divine in you.
I will celebrate you and not tolerate you.
I will work hard to make you feel capable and smart.
I will embrace the bad side and the good side in you.
Like me, you are looking for happiness, meaning and significance.
If I don't like you, I must get to know you.
I will value you by your best moments.
Since the air transmits what we feel, I will honor you in thought and speech.
We are all bad, but in different things.
I know you don't think you're bad.
I will look at your weakness with compassion, not accusation.
You have hurt me only to protect yourself; I will not take anything personally.
And when you hurt me, I know you are weak and incapable to will yourself to do better.
I may set boundaries and hold you accountable, but will always love you and aim to help you.

Release yourself from the cycle of constantly being hurt or offended. And encourage that practice among your team. Healthy leaders live beyond forgiveness.

Show Compassion: The Risk is Worth the Reward

If you want to excel in leadership, it is imperative that your people know and feel your genuine compassion toward them—all the time. Compassion in leadership simply communicates: *I care about your well-being.* And that caring is manifested in thoughts, words, and actions that clearly and consistently demonstrate it.

The first step to excelling in this area is very obvious, but the most difficult. You must truly and genuinely care about people's well-being. Here is the reality about people, about us. We are messy. People are messy. Caring about people is not for the faint of heart. It takes depth of character, sacrifice, and courage.

You may ask me, "But, why is it important to have compassion in *leadership*?"

Let me share with you how I feel about the leaders I follow. I want to be with people who care about my well-being. Don't you? I want my family, my friends, and my coworkers to care about me. And I certainly want the people who have authority over me to care. I want my mayor, senator, and president to care about my well-being.

The minute they do, and the more they do, the more loyalty, effort and dedication they will naturally get from me. The more I will follow them and support them.

Why? Because I know:

- They will not hurt me.
- They will not abuse me.
- They will not take advantage of me.
- They will care for me.
- They will nurture me.
- They will want the best for me.
- They will want my safety.
- They will want my happiness.
- They will care about my future.
- They will listen to my dreams.
- They will care about my health.
- They will care about my family.

Be bold enough to exercise compassion in your leadership. The risk is worth the reward.

Shhhhh…

The issue: You know the correct answer, the right question and the end game. So you go on talking, explaining and clarifying your position and perspective.

The problem: You actually *don't* know the correct answer, the right question, or the end game.

The solution: Be quiet. Quiet your lips, but more importantly your thoughts. As a leader, are you listening to discover what others think and see?

Shhhhh…Others may be right. *And you may be wrong.*

Leaders are naturally problem-solvers. Their minds (and often their mouths) instinctively leap into action in order to resolve issues. However, as I observe leaders seeking solutions, I consistently see them pontificating more than listening, lecturing more than receiving, moralizing, instructing and talking when they need to be quiet and look for ideas different from their own.

Even if they listen for a few seconds, but then jump in prematurely, their people often give up. It's just not worth it to team members to compete for a chance to talk. It hurts me to see these leaders hurt others and ultimately decrease their own capacity to lead when they talk and don't stop to truly listen. I think to myself, *Wow, if you could only be quiet and listen, the answer is staring you in the face.*

Are you being a good listener?

1. **Are you consistently inviting others to speak into your life (and meaning it)?** People don't like to barge in with advice. You can invite them by using phrases like these:

    - "I would like to invite you to speak the truth to me when you see me doing something wrong."

    - "You have my permission to tell me when you think I am off base."

2. **Are you creating the time and place for others to speak to you?** People will not speak what needs to be said in the wrong setting. Behind closed doors, or maybe after connecting on a personal level, is when most people will feel comfortable enough to speak.

3. **Are you insisting that they speak, and re-inviting them consistently?** If you want to hear from people, you have to constantly remind them of the invitation to speak, and reassure them that you will be okay with whatever they have to say.

4. **Are you punishing them when they speak?**
When people say something you don't like, are
you grateful or spiteful? Be careful that you are
not subliminally giving them signals not to
speak to you candidly, or they will stop.

5. **Are you inviting the right people to speak
into your life?** Invite those:

- Whom you trust. They will have no ulterior
motives.

- Who have successfully traveled before you.
They will give you sound advice.

- Who will not destroy you as they advise
you. Be cautious of reality-givers. Some are
simply too harsh. Their method destroys the
person, not just the idea. Seek those who
will help you see the reality without
crushing your hopes and dreams in the
process.

Be quiet. Just listen.

When people are speaking, don't defend your
position or talk too much. Rather, as the leader, *you*
choose to be quiet. Listen so you can see what they
see, feel what they feel, and think what they think.
Shhhhh…the key is to be quiet, and just listen.

Inspiration

chapter 6

Chief Complaint

MY STAFF IS NOT PERFORMING AT ITS BEST.

Prescription

RAISE PEOPLE TO A HIGHER LEVEL.

Lift People Up

God put a handful of people in your life—your team members, your boss, your family, your customers. Have you ever asked yourself, "What is my role in the life journey of these people?"

Do you use them to fill our needs, and occasionally give back so you don't feel selfish? Do you simply coexist with them in peace? Or, do you seek to make an enduring impact in their lives? Lifting people up is such a simple principle that it's easy to overlook and replace it with a "just be nice" approach to living.

Impart into others.

If you believe in God's divine will as I do, then you likely believe that it is His design for certain people to be in your life. My mentor, Pastor Peter Rahme, once told me, "God drops people in our laps." What an insightful way to look at people in our lives. They are not mere coincidences for us to interact with. Most of the time, most of us treat others with kindness and respect. We "live and let live." We live together and work together. We honor people and relationships. And that is good. Let me share with you, though, what is simply remarkable and life changing.

What if we don't see others merely as an employee, a spouse, or a customer? Could we say, *Wow, God put this person in my life for me to impact, to promote, to encourage, to increase, to love, to bless, and to add value to.* We could then begin to derive our success and satisfaction as leaders (and fellow human beings) from the privilege of knowing that this person was *brought into* our lives for us to powerfully pour into! What if those 10, 20, 30 people in your life become better people because they know you? Could they become more inspired, encouraged, motivated, or secure because of your influence?

But here's the kicker…what if they could give you *nothing* at all in return? Ever.

Lift others up, just because you should.

The trick to impacting people's lives is that we should not do it for the reward. We should do it just because we should. The only reward we should seek is the privilege of doing it. We will have had the chance to touch the life (in a big or small way) of one of God's children.

Here are some of the amazing things that can happen when we aim to lift others up. Remember, this is not to be our motivation for reaching others; this is just the icing on the cake.

1. People will come along with us.
2. People will truly care about us.
3. Our circle becomes healthy and happy.
4. We help create a culture of giving.
5. Our lives become filled with love and beauty, sincerity and humanity.

I have to remind myself of this most simple and powerful principle often. Commit to cherish and honor people—people whom God put into your life. Let's make it our goal to add value to them, consistently, intentionally, and aggressively.

Allow For Mistakes—
Even Big Ones

Over 150 years have passed since the Battle of Gettysburg in the United States' Civil War. 53,000 died in this epic battle. I have had the pleasure to visit the hallowed grounds of the Battle of Gettysburg twice. Each time I have taken time to sit and reflect at Cemetery Ridge, where that last and deciding assault took place on the afternoon of July third. Even though the Union won, Lincoln was not happy with the commanding general, George Meade, and he drafted a letter to him.

Meade's Failure

Pickett's Charge—named after one of the three commanding Southern generals, Major General George Pickett, who led the attack—included 12,500 soldiers who charged the Union lines. Its repulsion and the mass casualty of the Southern attackers of this frontal assault sealed the fate of the battle, and many think of the war, for the side of the Union.

The reason this frontal assault failed was in part because the artillery barrage from the Southern forces prior to the charge completely missed the Union lines and landed 200 to 300 yards behind where it was supposed to. One theory as to why this happened was because the Southern army was using a new factory for its gunpowder, which had a different explosive quality.

Even though the Southern army went to retreat after the failure of Pickett's charge, the Civil War lasted almost another two years. The reason, as President Lincoln and many others deduced, was because the Commanding Union General at Gettysburg, George Meade, decided not to pursue the retreating Southern army and force the surrender of the legendary General Robert E. Lee.

Lincoln's Response

President Lincoln was quite distressed by this lack of initiative, as he thought a final pursuit could have been the end of the war. He wrote a letter to General Meade that included this section:

> *Again, my dear General, I do not believe you appreciate the magnitude of the misfortune involved in Lee's escape. He was within your easy grasp, and to have closed upon him would, in connection with our other late successes, have ended the war. As it is, the war will be prolonged indefinitely. If you could not safely attack Lee last Monday, how can you possibly do so south of the river, when you can take with you very few more than two-thirds of the force you then had in hand? It would be unreasonable to expect, and I do not expect you can now affect much. Your golden opportunity is gone, and I am distressed immeasurably because of it.*

When I first read this letter, I was surprised as to the leniency of it. I thought, *I would have probably sent a stronger letter.*

What did General Meade think of it?

Nothing.

He never received it because President Lincoln never sent it. It was found in the effects of the President. Historians assume he did not send it because of the maturity of his leadership: a wise, patient, and highly effective approach...an approach not quick to condemn and criticize.

Mature leaders allow people to make mistakes—even big ones—without constantly correcting and criticizing, without making them feel small.

Help Your People Succeed In Life

Great leaders are more concerned with seeing their people succeed in life than they are with seeing them succeed as employees. This is a simple principle, yet one of the most powerful and difficult to live by when you are leading an organization or team.

Players of legendary sports teams commend their coaches for teaching them so much about how to live an honorable life beyond the field or the court.

Basketball great Kareem Abdul-Jabbar said of Coach John Wooden, "He wanted to win, but not more than anything...My relationship with him has been one of the most significant of my life...The consummate teacher, he taught us that the best you are capable of is victory enough, and that you can't walk until you crawl, that gentle but profound truth about growing up."

And another basketball legend, Larry Bird, described another coach, "Red Auerbach was one of the most influential people in my life. Not only was he an inspiration to me throughout my career, he became a close friend, as well. There could only be one Red Auerbach, and I'll always be grateful for having the opportunity to experience his genius and his dedication to winning through teamwork."

As a result of exceptional leadership, you see amazing loyalty, teamwork and success in such organizations. But more importantly, you see great humanity at work.

As leaders, how do we help people succeed in life?

While our exact definitions of success in life may differ, I think we could all agree it is a combination of being content, effective, productive and happy. It is having the ability to dream, grow and have a healthy balance between the pleasures, priorities and demands of life. So, how can we apply this practically as leaders?

- **Impact people's lives.** Know that to become a great leader, we should move from directing people's activities to impacting people's lives.

- **Do it for the right reason.** Work on caring about people's success in life because it is the right thing to do, and not as a trick to increase your influence.

- **Challenge, empower, and invest in people.** Give people the best you can to help them in the dance of life.

- **Don't become their psychotherapist.** Make yourself available to them in the role of a coach or mentor.

- **Listen to people.** Hear their heart! Know their dreams.

- **See their entire life.** Help them succeed in their current job, but this is not the entire story. Their entire life is the entire story— get to know it and be a positive part of it.

- **Do what is best for them, not for you.** Give people your best advice to help them move forward on their life journey, even if that sometimes means that it is not what is best for you. This is very important and will test your commitment to this principle. Put them first! (This includes letting them leave your team.)

On my own leadership journey, I reflect with sadness over those who moved on from my team whose lives were not positively touched. At the time, I simply was not good enough to impact them. Now, I am more committed than ever to the idea that if and when people leave my team, they leave as better human beings...bigger, kinder, and able do more and become more. But this is a commitment I have to often renew and remind myself of. I encourage you to do the same. Help your people succeed in life!

Push Someone Else Uphill

In July 2013, I participated in the RAGBRAI bicycling event in Iowa with my two brothers and our friend. It was the first time I had ever ridden in the event, which is a seven-day (50-80 miles per day) bike ride across Iowa from the west to east state lines. Tens of thousands of cyclists ride dangerously close together through the hills in the grueling heat. I learned a lot about navigating the rolling hills of Iowa—as well as the hills and valleys of leadership.

Bringing Others Alongside You

I witnessed many moments of humanity, teamwork, and leadership at its finest. The most touching scene of the race was of a father and daughter early in the ride. The entire race had a handful of young cyclists. This girl must have been about twelve years old, pedaling on her own bicycle next to her father.

I never met them, but as I rode closely behind them downhill, I noticed the girl had no issues. As we hit the bottom of the hill and began the next ascent, we all naturally started slowing down. Mid-hill she was slowing down more than her father, so he put his hand on her back. And as he rode beside her, he pushed her ever so gently, and she pedaled as hard as she could. Throughout the entire hill, he kept his hand behind her and she stayed with him alongside everyone else they were riding with.

Now, I am sure he did not have to bring her along. There were not many kids there. And even though I did not see them finish the entire ride, I can only imagine how a twelve-year-old would feel completing such a big ride! What a way to empower her, to make her feel accomplished and capable. And sure, she could have stopped and walked the hill. But he risked riding a hill with only one hand just to give her the thrilling feeling of conquering the steep and physically challenging incline.

Sacrificing a Little of Yourself

Even though that was the only hill I saw them riding, I am sure she got better and likely did not need his help on most ascents. But I know he was there for her because these kinds of people are always there for us—insisting that we come along, that we go the full journey with them. They are there in case we need them. And ever so gently, on the hills of our life journey, their hands are there to make sure we can make it.

Will you bring people up the hills of leadership with you? And when they fall behind, are you willing to sacrifice your speed to push them gently forward? Look for ways to lift people to a higher level, to gently push them, and to lead them. And watch their level of commitment and performance soar.

Teamwork

chapter 7

Chief Complaint

MY PEOPLE ARE NOT WORKING
WELL TOGETHER.

Prescription

TAKE A RELATIONAL APPROACH TO
TEAM BUILDING.

Build a Strong Team

Assembling a strong team should be a top priority for leaders. Those who have formidable teams experience the most success. Those who don't, often fail. If your team is fragmented and not working together as a cohesive unit, it is your responsibility to rise above the strife and pull people together. Here are a few key principles to help you with team leadership.

A Relational Approach to Team Building

1. **Make building and maintaining a great team a primary concern.** Give it priority in both your budget and your time. Focusing solely on results without properly caring for and maintaining your team is much like running a racecar at full-throttle toward the finish line without proper maintenance and pit stops. Stop and get a tune up!

2. **Assess your current team.** At what level is your team now?

   - Backstabbing and paralysis?
   - Gossiping and noncooperation?
   - Guarded coexistence and minimal coordination of efforts?
   - Supporting one another and producing good results?

- Oneness of spirit and effort, combined with creative excitement?

3. **Decide to take your team to the highest level and keep them there.** Make that decision and stick with it!

4. **Get training in teambuilding.** Read books and listen to seminars/webinars.

5. **Place people together who get along.** Do your best to predict who will potentially trust each other, get along and add strength to one another's weaknesses. Remove the rest.

6. **Start by making personal connections when possible.** Personal relationships are the key to a strong team. Begin setting the tone and modeling healthy relationships between team members.

7. **Now bring the team together.** Play, joke and spend time together. Work, plan and think together. Invite them to your home or ask them to volunteer together. One of my very favorite ways to bring a team together is to learn together. Get a book and read it weekly, for example.

8. **Review your organization's overall credos and cultural habits.** What are the mission and vision for your organization? More importantly what are the values of the organization? Do these promote teamwork or not, and what can you do to improve upon them?

A Noteworthy Impact on Your Organization

Don't underestimate the impact building a strong team can have on your clients and customers. A story is told of an owner of an Australian tire shop who purchased ingredients every Saturday morning to personally cook breakfast for his ten employees. His gesture was so appreciated by his staff, it created a culture of warmth all the way from the owner to the management to the employees... and straight to the customers. One such customer, Keith Ready[11], wrote:

> *As customers, we have an expectation that we will always receive good service from any business we deal with. However, what determines the quality of the customer service we receive is the attitude of the people who work in the business. As employees our attitudes toward what we do at work is influenced by many things, not least of all how our employer or boss treats us. What he was doing is rarely seen in business today. He was being of service to his team and setting an example by cooking them breakfast.*

If your people are not working well together, take ownership and exercise your leadership. Know that healthy leadership comes from the top down.

Seek Responsible People

Some people need constant reminding to get things done. They drain you, and you dread them. Others get things done even before you ask. They empower you, and you trust them. Where do you and your people rank on the following responsibility scale? And what are you doing about it?

Levels of Responsibility

Level 1: Need Pushing and Cajoling

We all know this group. They frustrate and demoralize us. They don't get things done unless you push, urge or cajole them. They may have poor time management skills or have completely lost motivation for one reason or another.

Level 2: Need Constant Reminders

This group is a little better, but not by much. They may not need to be pushed to get things done; however, they need constant reminding and gentle nudging.

Level 3: Need One Reminder

These people need one or two reminders; then they get their tasks done well.

Level 4: Need No Reminder

Now, this is the group that you want to hold onto. They always get the job done. You discuss with them what is needed, and it just gets done. Every time.

Level 5: They Get Things Done Without Being Told

This fifth level is a group of individuals who will get things done without you having to tell them. How will they know what needs to get done? By listening, learning, and discerning the mission, vision and values of the team. These are the people we should aim to have on our teams. They care, they drive, and they lead!

If you want to have a successful team, performers at the first two levels need to be removed. You should work to improve the third level performers. The last two levels are the ones you most want to have on your team. Don't settle for less!

Require Solutions

Have you ever been on teams where everyone is only discussing the problems? Where the air is toxic, negative and repulsive to any proactive, positive force? That's where a culture of blame and finger-pointing has been created.

When I insist that we avoid discussing problems on my teams, I often get this question: "How can we find fixes, if we don't find the faults first? We have to discuss the problems." And therein lies the excuse for a team's negative culture. People want to focus on the problem rather than focus on the solution. It is up to you as the leader to create a culture of that resists fault-finders and rewards solution-seekers.

I recently had a new employee come to me and say that she would like to have an open time during our team meeting to present some problems, to "discuss them" with the team. Sounds benign and healthy, doesn't it?

I said, "No. We will not discuss problems. We will discuss solutions." As she gave me a perplexed look, I said, "I love the fact that you want to address problems. Bring the problems and your proposed solutions to me, and then as a group we will discuss the *solutions* to the problems and not the problems."

That employee still did not understand. She was so used to having an open floor to ramble on discussing problems. As the leader, you have to stand firm to not allow this, or else your team's culture will slide into the abyss.

Think about it: you don't have to be especially intelligent, experienced, or wise to simply find a fault, mistake, or a problem. People do it all the time. But, it takes a person of character, experience, and intelligence to find solutions. And, it takes a real leader to see it through. Identifying a problem is only the first step toward arriving at a solution. Create a solution-seeking culture.

Let It Go—Some People Just Cannot Be Harmonized

Early in my leadership journey, I was always eager to create harmony in the workplace—a culture of cooperation, respect, hard work, and camaraderie in the teams I led. After all, this was my responsibility, and I took it seriously.

Some teams worked together so easily, and it was amazing to be a part of that experience. However, I faced situations in other teams where two or more people on my team did not get along, even with my very best efforts—gentle suggestions, stern talks, teambuilding activities, or creating a fun environment—nothing worked. It hampered the effectiveness of the team. And I always blamed myself for that. After all, this was my team, and if people did not work together and connect well, my team was suboptimal. And I believed I was to blame.

A Simple Discovery

I made a simple discovery that helped me process this failure and move past it. I read somewhere that the job of a leader is to *create a coordination of efforts in a spirit of harmony...and that some people simply cannot be harmonized.*

Cannot? At first I refused to accept that. I was a firm believer in the ability of people to grow (and I still am). I told myself, "I will inspire them and love them so much that they will transcend their inability to work in a spirit of harmony. They will want to do it for the team. If not, they will do it for my sake."

Sometimes this worked, and sometimes it just did not. After more time passed, and as I did more thinking, writing, praying, leading, failing, and trying—I surrendered to the idea…

Some people just cannot be harmonized.

But be careful here. This is not an excuse for us as leaders to throw in the towel and not work to encourage, cajole, or even to push people to learn to connect and get along. Creating harmony in the workplace requires a positive, uplifting culture that brings out the best in people.

A Conscious Connection

Remember these principles in teambuilding:

- People will not interact in harmony with everyone.

- When forming a team, choose people who you have natural harmony with.

- Choose team members who have harmony between each other.

- Work hard to help your team form relationships that are bathed in love, camaraderie, and self-sacrifice. Model it.

- If you find yourself with people who cannot interact in harmony after intentional time and effort to bring them together (I usually give us a few months), then I encourage you to move on. (Move them away from each other right away.)

When it becomes clear that harmony is not achievable, move on from blaming yourself and pushing others to "just get along," to accepting that some people just cannot be harmonized. When that happens, team members may need to be moved—or removed.

Align Your Efforts
as a Team

In July 2013, I had the incredible opportunity to participate in RAGBRAI: a 7-day (50 to 80 mile per day) bike ride across the state of Iowa from the western to eastern state lines.

My experience bicycling at RAGBRAI stretched me in so many ways. During the hours and hours of riding each day, I witnessed many things that grew my understanding of teamwork and leadership.

Expose your team to challenging experiences.

Our small team consisted of amateur cyclists. In fact all four of us (my two brothers, our friend, and myself) bought our road bikes about five weeks before RAGBRAI. Our muscles, lungs, and coordination were nowhere close to where they needed to be. Each morning, all the participants took to the roads, which were blocked to cars by the state troopers. We rode alongside hundreds of cyclists at any given time. As the day progressed and the experienced riders sped ahead, the mass of cyclists spread out onto the expanse of the road and the congestion thinned out. It was fascinating to me to observe how the veteran bikers rode together in a seamless fashion on teams. They seemed to ride faster and to be having a lot of fun together. That was not at all what we looked like!

These teams were like a finely tuned and synchronized dance. Most were about eight to twelve people, riding two by two behind each other. The front two teammates set the pace and the rest kept up, pedaling consistently. Pedaling with purpose and resolve. It was as if they drew energy from each other. They seemed focused and on target. Many of them had one member of the team with a music boom box either attached to their bicycle or pulled behind it and powered by solar panels or large batteries. These groups always zoomed by while the rest of us struggled. I am sure it was not their first time fighting through it together. I am sure they practiced often as a team.

Traverse the course as a team.

Leading *with* your team is so much more effective than leading out front on your own. As leaders, sometimes we forget the power of having a coherent team with us. We start thinking too highly of ourselves. We start wanting to go it alone, and only on occasion to go with others. Often times we have not been intentional to truly work together— not just to coexist. Other times we find we are simply not moving together, synchronizing our efforts. We forget that a symphony can only be produced by a group of people in agreement and in harmony. Wherever your journey leads, traverse the course together as a team.

Leadership

chapter 8

Chief Complaint

I DON'T LIKE DEALING WITH CONFLICT.

Prescription

REFUSE TO AVOID THE MESSY BUSINESS
OF PEOPLE.

Deal with Issues, Lead People

Most people who write and speak about leadership paint a picture of the leader and the people as a beautiful symphony of love and passion. That may be true…10% of the time. The rest of the time, a leader has to deal with personnel issues, with at least one person on the team, sometimes a few, and occasionally everyone.

At any one point, you may have to deal with someone with…

- a poor attitude
- low productivity
- low motivation
- low integrity
- the habit of negative talk
- slow intellect
- inability to focus
- unwillingness to grow
- unwillingness to lead
- a need to rebel
- a desire to destroy
- a rude demeanor
- disrespectful language
- an unprofessional appearance
- unprofessional behavior
- slowness to move
- unwillingness to change

Dealing with Issues

In all my years of leadership, I can hardly recall a time when I was not dealing with issues like these. Some issues are small, some are big, and some are unbearably painful. Leadership is a messy business! If you are not careful, it can keep you up at night, and send you into bouts of depression and worry. Even one of the most astute leaders, President Lincoln, suffered with the demands of leadership. Why? Because understanding, aligning, and keeping a group of people focused and passionate is simply difficult.

You have to be a psychologist, a counselor, an encourager, an inspirer, a parent, a teacher. You have to be a fair judge and a hard worker, willing to sacrifice, able to bite your tongue and bend your pride. You have to have courage, empathy, vision, character, patience, and forgiveness. And you have to have love—for all!

You have to know who to hire, who to promote, who to let go, who to discipline, who to write up, who to speak to gently, who to speak to sternly. You have to know how to keep Human Resources happy, how to avoid offending people, and not break any laws—all while keeping a motivated and disciplined team.

Leading People

Leaders are in the business of people, and it is a difficult business. But, it is the most honorable business you can be in. We are in the business of love, of dreams, and of great accomplishments. Whether you are a parent, a team member, a manager, or a president, if you are committed to being a great leader, then you have committed to leadership's hardest yet most rewarding challenge...*people.*

Resist the Urge to Demand Respect

What can you do when your people don't respect you? As a leader, it's easy to fall into the trap of thinking you can demand respect. Being assertive may temporarily cause people to leap into action. But reaction to your commands does not necessarily equal respect for your authority. Demanding respect from your people does nothing to foster trust and build relationships. In fact, it usually makes you look like a fool. So as a leader, how can you obtain the respect of your people without indulging in harsh and demeaning behaviors?

Never give an order that you don't know will be obeyed.

The boisterous and outright aggressive general of World War II, General Douglas MacArthur, said, "Never give an order that can't be obeyed." Of course, I don't like the words *order* or *obey* in the context of leadership, but there is a message here I believe we can learn from. Think about it, a formidable Army general has to premeditate the orders he gives, how they will be received, and if they will be followed. As leaders in businesses and organizations, shouldn't we too consider the repercussions of our requests?

Before you ask people to help you with something, you need to know them well enough to know whether they will feel good about doing it. Can they do it? Would they want to do it? Do they like to do it? While those criteria should not prevent you from delegating responsibility, understanding those factors can help you deal with a variety of challenges that may arise.

Ask people to help you. Don't tell them to do it.

Strong leadership is gentle leadership. Here are a few respectful ways to request action from your people:

- Can I have you help me with this?

- Would you mind taking care of this?

- When you have a moment, could you help me with this?

Now you may say, "When I say that, my people treat me as if I am begging, as if they have the power." If you are at that stage in the relationship, one of two things is the issue:

1. The boundaries are not well defined, or

2. The relationship is in the tank.

And both of these can and should be fixed right away, one-on-one. But, the bottom line is this: you should not constantly be in a position where you

- Have them work with someone else with whom they do connect. (Although this can be dangerous—you don't want to use this as an excuse to dump bad players on other leaders because you don't want to deal with their issues.)

- If all else fails, remove them from my team.

In dealing with people, refrain as much as possible from forcing issues by being assertive. Rather, lead people. Win their respect by developing relationships with them one-on-one. And recognize that on occasion you will encounter someone who just cannot be reached. And that is okay.

A good leader is like an artist delicately painting on canvas. As a painter, if you cannot be careful, delicate and most importantly patient—for example, if you cannot wait for your colors to dry for the next day—you will have a mess on your hands! Patiently work with people one-on-one, and over time you will create beautiful work together.

Do Not Tolerate Bad Attitudes

Having a bad attitude, or allowing a culture of bad attitudes, will kill your team. They should not be tolerated among your organization, your team, your church, or your family.

Do you know anyone with a bad attitude?

You know, they hardly smile, are quick to complain, talk about others, gossip and murmur. You ask them "How are you?" They answer apathetically, "I'm here," or "I've had better days." And there is always something wrong. Always. When you talk to them, they will answer but after a five to ten second delay. They are short and snippy. They are resentful and revengeful. They act like they feel the whole world owes them something. They are convinced that people are out to get them. They don't like to play by the rules, and they support the vision grudgingly.

Do you know anyone like that? As a leader, how do you handle these people? Honestly, I'd like to shake them and plead with them to wake up! I want to tell them, "Hey buddy, you are not the only one with problems. Get over yourself." Or, "You are dragging this whole team down." I'd like to think that professionalism and being an adult mean that you keep your problems in check.

Of course I don't do any of these things. But as I stop and think about all of this, I cannot escape the fact that—yes, I admit it—sometimes I am *that person.* I shouldn't feel entitled as the leader to judge and criticize those with a bad attitude, until I reflect and improve upon my own.

If you find that *you* are the one with the bad attitude, what steps can you take to turn it around? The most important step, I believe, is to know what a good attitude looks like. Only then can you do something about it.

Thomas Jefferson said, "Nothing on earth can help the man with the wrong mental attitude."

What does a good attitude look like?

I believe a good attitude is being…

- **Joyful,** not sad.
- **Hopeful,** not hopeless.
- **Helpful,** not self-seeking.
- **Grateful,** not selfish.
- **Delighted,** not gloomy.
- **Excited,** not indifferent.
- **Passionate,** not apathetic.
- **Vibrant,** not lethargic.
- **Forgiving,** not resentful.
- **Believing,** not doubtful.
- **Encouraging,** not disheartening.
- **Rising above it all,** not getting stuck in the hurt.
- **Content,** not despondent.

- **Alive this very moment,** not agonizing.
- **Optimistic,** not cynical.
- **Persistent,** not flaky.
- **Patient,** not frustrated, irritated, or exasperated.
- **Confident,** not doubtful or afraid.
- **Calm,** not panicked.
- **Smiling,** not frowning.

Improve attitudes within your team.

Why do so many teams have people with bad attitudes? Because leaders allow it! They tolerate it in the name of "patience" or "being understanding." They think that it is a normal part of a team. Big mistake. As a leader, I want you to know the following:

1. Consistently having bad attitude is not normal, and it is not okay.

2. A bad attitude in one member of your team will make your entire team dysfunctional and ineffective. It will make your team mediocre, because communication gets stifled and energy is spent in dealing with the bad attitude instead of forward progress.

3. It is your responsibility as a leader to deal with it. When I see a team where someone consistently has a bad attitude, I blame one person—the leader. Many times that has been me. In those times, I was unwilling or unable to deal with or remove the person with the bad attitude. The whole team suffered because I failed as a leader.

4. Hire for skill and attitude. We usually hire for skill. We mostly want to make sure a person can do the job. But do we pay attention to see if a person can fit into a team? Can they maintain a good attitude when things do not go their way?

5. Fire for attitude. Skill can be taught. Attitude usually cannot. The faster the person with a bad attitude is off your team, the faster your team can heal and grow.

6. You may be the cause of everybody's bad attitude. If everyone on your team has a bad attitude, it is worth asking if you are the problem. Are you the one that needs to move on? Or are you the person with the bad attitude?

7. Nurture, love, and empower, but don't make excuses for a bad attitude. This has been a challenge for me. I naturally tend to nurture and empower people. I also tend to make excuses for their bad attitudes. Big mistake. I have learned to move past this quality and be serious with offenders in this area.

8. Don't keep someone with a bad attitude because they have a great skill. Most of the time as leaders, we think it is better to keep someone with a great skill even if they have a bad attitude. The truth is that as a leader I can do ten times more with a team that gets along, even if they have less skill, than with a team that has great skill, but does not get along and is full of drama.

9. The most important job of a leader is to induce coordination of effort in a spirit of harmony. If your team is running wild, not getting along, not working together, where poor attitude and drama is the culture, and you cannot induce harmony, you simply need to resign your post. You are not doing your basic job as a leader.

10. People learn from each other. People have a tendency to adopt the attitudes of those they spend time with—to pick up on their mind-sets, beliefs, and approaches to challenges. Bad attitudes can and do spread among your team members.

Tolerating a bad attitude versus dealing with it directly distinguishes an effective leader from an ineffective leader. I can tell you from personal experience that bad attitudes are not easy to deal with. But for the sake of our teams, we must.

Lead the Hard to Influence

As a leader, what do you do with the difficult to lead? It may be your spouse, your child, your team member, your employee or your boss! A few years ago, I was approached by one of our managers with a question I think every good leader asks. She said, "How do I influence the hard to influence on my team—you know, those that you just can't reach?"

I thought to myself, *Wow, isn't this is the dilemma of every leader?* I did not respond with an answer right away, but asked if I could take a few days to think on it. In the weeks that followed, we had a dialogue about this important topic. But that question has been with me ever since, and I ask it of myself often.

"What's wrong with them?"

When we encounter someone who is hard to influence, we usually ask ourselves, "What's wrong with them? If only they would see it. If only they would wise up. If only they would come along." We get frustrated, irritated and bent out of shape. Here is what's wrong with them: nothing.

It's about what's wrong with you and me. That's the problem. We are focused on the wrong person. The difficult lesson I learned is this: If I were a better leader, they would come along. The sooner we understand this very simple principle, the sooner we will start moving mountains, influencing people and going to great places with them. But this is a difficult principle to understand and apply.

Great leaders know this. They know that it's not up to people to change so they can see how great we are, how great the vision is, or how great our ideas are. It is up to us to change so we can have an impact on them.

Can the hard to influence even be reached?

If Jesus had a weak vision, did not sacrifice, did not love, did not train others, or did not empower the twelve disciples, not too many would have followed Him. Many who were influenced would have remained hard to influence.

If Martin Luther King, Jr., did not dream, did not march, did not insist on human dignity, and did not die for his cause, not too many would have followed him. Many who were influenced would have remained hard to influence.

If Mother Teresa did not suffer for her cause, did not have a depth and breadth to her character, and did not have a commitment to her mission, not too many would have followed. Many who were influenced would have remained hard to influence.

To gain traction with people, remember it's more about changing ourselves than others. If we understand people better, if we empower them more, if we are very clear on our expectations, if we inspire them, if we share with them our passion and vision, if we model sacrifice and giving, they may not be difficult to lead after all. There is a key to every heart. As leaders, it is our job to find it.

Create Relationships
That Thrive

Excellent leadership.
Flourishing families.
Enviable marriages.
Thriving organizations.
Effective teams.

They all have one factor in common: healthy relationships. We ache when we have bad ones. We celebrate when we have good ones. So how do we keep our relationships healthy?

The (not so) secret ingredient to any relationship in your life is time. To destroy a relationship, stop spending *consistent, quality* time with that person. To build lasting, meaningful relation-ships, start spending *consistent, quality* time with that person. It's that simple.

Think about a relationship you have right now that is simply not working. It's in an unacceptable state. There may be yelling, snipping, or silence. Someone may even be manipulating or intentionally harming another. And you may be thinking as you read this: *this is going to require more than just time. This relationship needs a miracle!* Well, you are right. If you are at that stage, you may need a God-size miracle. But I can guarantee that at some point in the past you ignored a fundamental tenant of relationship building: spending quality time with the other person.

Even if you are at a hopeless state, the advice below can still prove very beneficial in turning this relationship around. Whether it be personal or professional in nature, if you are to rebuild a failing relationship or grow a thriving one—*consistent, quality* time will be an integral part of your journey with that person. Here are some ideas on how to strengthen your relationship to a point that it is thriving.

8 Steps to Building and Maintaining Thriving Relationships

1. **Take responsibility for the relationship.** Most of us start to work on a relationship by solving issues. While that is certainly important, there is actually a better first step: Stop solving issues, start making a connection. Stop pointing a finger, and start building bridges. Stop waiting for something to happen, and start taking the initiative. Stop focusing on your wounds, and start looking for the answers. If a relationship in your life is not working, or you wish for it to work better, you must take the lead (without announcing that you are doing so).

2. **Give the relationship priority**. Building healthy relationships requires time. If you don't have time, you are simply not giving

this relationship priority. We all have tewnty-four hours in a day. You are spending those hours on something else. If you are still not convinced, let me put it to you this way. Do you want to have a failed business? Ignore relationships. Do you want to have a failed marriage? Ignore relationships. Do you want to have a failed team? Ignore relationships. Relationships are the cornerstone for success in your life, my friend. *Give them priority!*

3. Consistently spend quality time together.

This is not rocket science. Consistently, carve out time specifically to spend together. There will always be other demands on our time. So, figure it out. Find a time during your busy schedule. Make time to talk to your employees. Hire a babysitter. Arrange for a peer to cover your shift at work. *Make* it happen. How much time? Enough time that you can see the human side of each other. Enough time that you finish talking about *business* and start talking about life. Among the important relationships and teams in my life, and especially if there is a high level of stress involved, I apply this principle: short daily meetings and longer weekly meetings. Yes, I meet daily with some people for a short time (10 to 15 minutes), and longer if we only meet weekly (30 to 60 minutes).

4. **Be consistent.** Friend, don't wait until there is tension. Keep the relationship bank full. You will have to work much harder to repair the damage when you are not consistent, or just spend time together when there is tension. Make a schedule and stick to it.

5. **Quality means quality.** You cannot have quality time unless you are fully present. Turn off your cell phone if you have to. Go offsite if you must. Stop, and really listen. Engage. Be alone with that person. Quality time means that the world needs to disappear when the two of you connect.

6. **Investing time leads to breaking down walls.** Spending time together creates a solid foundation. But that's not the final step. The goal of spending time together is for barriers between the two of you to crumble and fall away. And that almost always happens when you spend *consistent, quality* time together. When two people start seeing the human side of each other, hearts soften, and walls start coming down. And as your relationship progresses, new walls don't get built.

7. **Be patient and gentle.** When you start spending *consistent, quality* time with a person, don't demand that they open up. Each person has a different comfort level when it comes to revealing their heart. I know people who are quick to bare it all. And I know people who bottle it in and never do. Be respectful. Be kind. We are all

trying to make it in life. You don't know what's going on inside the heart of another person. Remember that the strongest force in the world is gentleness.

8. **Practice honesty.** Once you are spending *consistent, quality* time together, and you are being patient and gentle with one another, there's one last step. Know what you want to say, but don't say it yet. That's right, wait for the right time. But don't wait too long; make sure it is expressed.
Somehow, you must communicate how you feel. Tell people when they cross a boundary. Let your relationship bank become so full, that when you make an *honesty* withdrawal, you are not left overdrawn. When candor exceeds connection, relationships start breaking down. Don't be afraid to be candid. Almost anything can be said in the right time and in the right way.

Here is the truth. Even for the best of us, some relationships are tough to manage. We must strive to have the best relationships because most of our successes, failures, pains, and joys come from the relationships we have. Healthy ones heal us, and oppressive ones suffocate us. Loving, uplifting ones build us, and give us life and strength. Toxic ones poison us. Make time to invest into your relationships. When you give people your time, they will give you their hearts.

Perseverance

chapter 9

Chief Complaint

I FEEL DEFEATED.

Prescription

USE FAILURE AS A SPRINGBOARD FOR GROWTH.

Succeed at Trying

Freed Zakaria, of CNN's GPS ("Global Public Square"), conducted an inspiring interview with Sara Blakely, the founder of Spanx, a highly successful undergarment company. In 2012, at the age of 41, Sara Blakely was named the world's youngest self-made female billionaire by *Forbes* magazine.[12]

During the course of this interview she recounted how as a fax machine sales person with a tenacious drive and $5,000 in savings, she took an idea she believed in and started a company that now makes $500 million in annual revenue. What's even more astounding is that she has had no outside investors, and she owns 100% of her company.

Defining Failure

What really got my attention was not the rags-to-riches story. It was toward the end of the interview when Fareed asked her what she credits most for her success. Her answer made me reach for my remote and rewind several times to take notes. She said it was her dad and the way he encouraged her *to fail.* Sara said,

> *My dad at the dinner table would ask my brother and me what we had failed at that week. And if we did not have a story to tell him he would actually be disappointed. And I can distinctly remember coming home and saying, 'Dad! Dad! I tried out for this and I*

*was horrible.' And he's high-fiving me and saying, 'Way to go!' And so what happened was, he reframed my thinking on failure. So **failure for me became: 'not trying' versus 'not succeeding.'** And I think, more than anything, what stifles entrepreneurship and risk-taking, is that all these people are sitting on million-dollar ideas for fear of failure. And so that was a real big gift I got from the way I was raised.*

What a powerful lesson. What a wise parent. I've read several books on how a healthy understanding of failure can be life changing, like John Maxwell's *Failing Forward*. [13] Sara really brought it home for me in a personal way as I listened to how this advice came from a father to his young children. So as a leader (and parent) here are some practical thoughts for you about failure.

Identifying Success

- If you have children, you have an amazing opportunity to impact their lives. First, I believe you do that by growing yourself. I don't know much about Sara's dad, but he must be a person of wisdom. If he had not discovered this healthy understanding of failure, and most likely practiced it, he would not have been able to teach it to his daughter. The best way to help your child is to grow yourself.

- Good failure is when you try and fail. Failure due to laziness and lack of effort is bad failure. Getting an "F" on your exam because you stayed up late watching TV the last few nights instead of studying is bad failure. Getting an "F" in organic chemistry while giving it your best effort is good failure. That is exactly what Sarah's dad taught her. Not trying is failure. Not succeeding is not necessarily failure.

- As part of my personal growth, I allocate time to just ask myself some key questions. One of them is, "What did I try and fail at today? And what can I learn from it?" After listening to this interview, I redoubled my efforts to ask this question more often.

- Make sure you stop and learn something from failure. If you keep repeating the same failure, that is also bad failure. Good failure is when you try something new, fail, and learn. Then you are ready to try again, hopefully with better results.

It is said that failure is life's way of nudging you onto another path. Keep trying new things, until you succeed at any one thing. I want to challenge you to keep daring to fail!

Remain Solid Under Pressure

If you recall from your high school or college chemistry class, each substance has three states: solid, liquid, and gas. As temperature is increased, each substance reaches its own melting point and subsequently its own boiling point.

> *melting point:* the temperature at which a substance changes from a solid to a liquid
> *boiling point:* the temperature at which a substance changes from a liquid to a gas

What are your melting and boiling points?

1. At what temperature (as induced by stress, problems, tension, or drama) do you melt? How much pressure and stress does it take for you to cave in, melt down, become liquefied and unable to keep it together?

2. At what temperature do you boil over? How much heat can you withstand before you become emotional, uncontrolled or erratic, operate in anger or in a hysterical mode of thinking or acting?

During a 2004 interview, former Chief Justice of the United States, William Rehnquist, was asked which personal qualities had caused him to excel in his position. At this point in his career, he had served over a decade as a Chief Justice, and was very highly regarded in the country and on the Supreme Court.

After thinking on the question briefly, he smiled and said that his passive nature and high boiling point were keys to his success. He said staying calm and unruffled was imperative in leading eight other highly intelligent and independently thinking individuals in adjudicating complex and infinitely consequential court cases.

When the temperature gets higher for us, we naturally deploy a set of skills and habits as a means to cope with the pressure. We combat stressful situations with a set of default patterns of thoughts and emotions.

Would you react with the grace of this man?

In 1873 prominent American lawyer Horatio Spafford lost his four daughters as a ship carrying them and his wife sank on the way to England. She sent the now famous telegraph, "Survived alone." He sailed to England to meet his grieving wife. Passing the point where the doomed ship had sunk, Spafford wrote the beloved hymn, "It Is Well With My Soul," demonstrating his deeply grounded faith.

When peace like a river
attendeth my way;
When sorrows like sea billows roll;

Whatever my lot, Thou hast taught me to say,
It is well, it is well, with my soul.

Can you withstand the heat and pressure?

What does it take for you or me to "lose it?" What does it take to make us emotionally distraught? To give up? What pushes us over the edge? Just like the substances in chemistry class, the melting points and boiling points are unique for all of us. And they change as we traverse the landscape of life, hopefully increasing as we grow and develop. The person who can withstand the heat is the one who has developed foundational principles that can be employed at a moment's notice. This person has adopted codes, beliefs, and values that are brought to bear when the temperature soars.

It is not a coincidence that the greatest business people, world leaders, and those of high esteem are solid—especially when the heat is on. Nelson Mandela was in prison for 27 years and remained *solid,* coming out to lead his country against tyranny. Martin Luther King, Jr., was imprisoned and constantly threatened but stayed *solid.*

It takes a temperature of 5,084 degrees Fahrenheit to cause gold to boil over. As the temperature rises on us as leaders, may we dedicate ourselves to dig deep and continually develop the character that will keep us from boiling over. May we aim to be like solid gold: able to withstand incredible heat and remain beautiful under pressure.

Confront Failure

If you live a life of leadership, an intentional journey to take people places, you will fail at some point—sometimes repeatedly, sometimes hard, and sometimes gravely. At times I wonder how a high-profile CEO feels when he's fired. Or, how does a high-level leader feel when the company he or she is leading is in severe decline? We hear about such events often in the news.

I seriously don't think these leaders are not trying, doing their best, or giving it all they've got. I am sure they get the best consultants, read the latest books, and do their due diligence. I have no doubt they have worked hard their entire career, and garnered immense knowledge and acumen. I would imagine they have won personal battles and developed character that is tested by fire. So what should we do when we have given it our very best, and yet we still fail?

Failing in Leadership

Daniel Hesse, the CEO of Sprint since 2007, has presided over an 80% drop in the value of his company's stock. He was featured on the list of Worst CEO's of 2012 by CNBC. I have never met Daniel, but I commiserate with him. Don't get me wrong, I would not cut him any slack—and I am sure he would not cut himself any slack either. He is the leader of that company, and he is responsible.

I commiserate with him because I know that often times as a leader, you do your very best, you apply all the principles you know, all the tricks in your bag. You talk to all the smart people around you, but you still fail. It may be at home, failing to lead your children well. As a doctor, I see so many parents, devastated as they lose their children to drugs and violence. Sometimes I ask myself, "Did this parent not try to impact and discipline their kids?" But I quickly answer myself, "Of course they did. They did their best."

Maybe you've experienced failure as a team leader. Perhaps there is a person on your team you just cannot reach. You've tried everything—the nice, the firm, the carrot, the stick—and nothing works. We could ask ourselves why good, diligent, hard-working people fail as leaders. But maybe it's better to accept that regardless of how good leaders become, they are not immune to failure. Perhaps the better question for us to ask ourselves is, "What should we do when we fail as leaders?"

10 Actions to Take in the Face of Failure

1. **Redouble your efforts to grow intentionally as a leader.** It is simply astounding to me how many people I meet who are failing in leading their marriages, their kids, their teams, and their organizations—and still refuse to intentionally grow. I ask them, "Are you doing anything to grow in that area? Are you reading books to grow?" The

answer is almost always "no." I beseech you, don't let that be you.

2. **Cut yourself some slack.** It is okay. Take a deep breath. Failure does not mean that you are a horrible person. Failure means that your current skillset and/or the contributing circumstances simply could not lead to a better result. If you had different (or better) skills, or if the circumstances were different, the result could have been better.

3. **Honor people's dignity.** This is something you should never fail at. I never, ever want to fail at it. I may fail at not being able to build a great team, show a great profit, or lead my organization to the limelight. As much as I try, as much as I grow, and as much as I become, there will be situations I simply cannot handle. But honoring people's humanity, and showing them dignity is a must. Let people say that about you, always. Let them say, "Above all, he loved me."

4. **Face the music.** When you fail, admit it. When you do, you can move on, you can look for different solutions, different people to lead, and different approaches to apply. When things are not working, it is admirable to try, try, and try harder, but only to a point. When it is clear you are not able to push through, stop. Think. Redirect. Re-strategize. So many of us try harder when we just need to stop and try *differently*.

5. **Listen to people.** Look for the critics. Obviously the ones who have told you that you are

doing well were wrong. You are failing. So, listen to all the opposing views now with an open mind.

6. **Listen to your heart.** So many of us fail because we simply do not listen to our gut, our intuition, our instinct. Have the courage to make that an integral part of your decision making.

7. **Be happy you know your limit.** Failure means that you've pushed yourself outside your current skillset and your comfort zone. Now you know your limit. You know what you need to work on.

8. **Define success properly.** What is success for you? Is it great results? Is it great profit? Is it great kids? Is it having a great organization? Is it winning the game? Or the championship? I do not think success should be defined as such. And defining success properly is key for us when we face failure. Because failing at what is important is different than failing at what is peripheral. For me, success is that we grow daily, conquer ourselves, try our best, give consistently, and plant great seeds in others. In the movie *Braveheart*, William Wallace dies at the end, and the rebellion is crushed. But we all think he was a success. He gave his 100% effort. So should we. And that should be our goal and our reward— knowing that we gave it all we had.

9. **Stand up to life.** My mother gave me the best simple advice many years ago—advice only a mother can give. I was feeling down because of a setback in my career. She looked at me and said, "Son, you have to be stronger than life." Life can

crush you. Stand up tall! Decide to face whatever challenges you have. When you cower down, you will be run over. I have no doubt about it. Life has no mercy sometimes.

10**. Be humble.** Have you considered that it's possible that what you are doing is wrong? I don't care if you are applying things that led to success previously, and you *know* they are the right things to try. You could be dead wrong in the way you are thinking, acting, feeling, working, or leading. Being humble means that you let go forever of feelings of infallibility.

We are so sure our way, our religion, our thinking, our actions, our parenting, our leadership, our political views, our communication is just right. Let me break it to you…if it were so right, you would not be at a point of failure today. You are a human being. Your ancestors and mine were just as smart as we are, and they thought that slavery was an acceptable way of living, that the earth was flat, and that drilling a hole in the skull was the best way treat a severe migraine. We have got to let go of this attitude of infallibility, if we are to begin seeing solutions we've never seen before.

I know you may be hurting now because of failure. Take heart; you are in good company. We all fail. We all have that in common. But it is what we do when we fail that will differentiate us.

Never Give Up

Anytime I push myself outside of my comfort zone, things get tough. When I operate in the areas I am not as familiar with, I often miss when I fire. I over-commit, I over-promise, or I over-estimate. I under-perform, I under-prepare, or I under-deliver. Why? Because when I get outside of my comfort zone, I am not as knowledgeable, intuitive, or capable. The ground becomes dangerously shaky, and the clouds become dark. I doubt myself. I want to quit.

In those dark moments, when things are closing in on us, when we have given it our very best and cannot give any more, that very moment of despair in our heart of hearts when we know we have gone astray…we want to give up. Don't.

I have wanted to quit.

As I look back at my life, many moments have passed when I felt this way. Many times I simply wanted to quit. As I have grown older, and have had more life experience, I still feel this way.

I felt this way as a teenager when I was about to get on stage at a piano competition, and I had just come from the bathroom because I got sick from being so nervous. I felt this way during my residency after I had been up for 23 hours, and I could not keep my eyes open any longer. I felt this way when I started a business and it failed, and I let people down. I felt this way when I flew off the handle talking to an employee when I should have been calm. I felt this way last week, when I questioned why I was writing articles and books when I could be resting from a long day at work.

For those moments when you want to give up, I want to tell you: *it's okay*. You are human, and I want to give you some ideas to help you continue in the fight.

I found the formula for pressing in.

What we need most in these moments of defeat is resolve. We need to muster a sense of resolve from deep inside that will carry us through. How do we find our strength and resolve?

Resolve = Passion + Purpose + Discipline

Passion gives you fire.

Purpose gives you direction.

Discipline gives you focus.

I've found that when your passion is alive, your purpose is defined, and your discipline is ready, you can weather any storm and scale any mountain. So, when you want to give up, do this instead:

1. **Renew your passion**. What makes you tick? What gets you excited? What gives you energy? When do you come alive and filled with life and love and fire? *Guide your life there.*

2. **Revisit your purpose**. What is the purpose of your life? What is the one thing you want to accomplish above anything else? What is it you want to be? What is the one destination you want to arrive at before you leave this planet? *Guide your life there.*

3. **Sharpen your discipline**. What keeps you on board? What keeps you focused? What helps you stay centered and consistent? Who keeps you motivated and accountable? *Guide your life there.*

When you feel like you've had enough, and you are ready to give up, reignite the fire that started it all. Renew your passion. Revisit your purpose. Sharpen your discipline.

Guard Your Heart

As a leader, you are always dreaming and pushing—and if you are like me, sometimes cracking under the weight of responsibility you put yourself under. Ambitious tendencies often get in the way of an immensely important area that you should never ignore—the condition of your heart. Having a healthy heart should be our number one priority.

Do you ever get into seasons in your life when you run yourself into the ground? You focus on your lofty ideals and goals, as well as your God-given purpose, but then forget your own heart. You find yourself empty and unable to give any more. And you become unhinged.

A Healthy Heart

Can you think of the times when you feel at peace, centered, fulfilled, confident, passionate, and focused? You know, those times when you are able to love more deeply, forgive more, and lead better. The times when you are not short-tempered, irritable, or confused. The times when you sleep soundly, don't rush through life, and are productive and focused.

I am not talking about being happy, or even content. Go beyond that. I am talking about when regardless of what is happening *to* you, what is happening *in* you is so mystically beautiful and strong that you can withstand life and all its storms.

A healthy heart should always be our top priority. Not for selfish reasons, but because that is how we honor our humanity and are able to give the most.

A Fulfilled Heart

As a physician, owner of a busy business, and participant in several ventures I started or support, I admit that I often easily slip into seasons when my life purpose and my passions take over my life. As the demands consume my spirit, I often ask myself what I must do to keep my heart filled.

I made a list of a few areas that truly fill my heart. They are simple, but always work when I am disciplined to do them daily. Yours may be different, but I would like to share mine with you. They are:

1. Reading

2. Time with God

3. Personal Growth

4. Exercise

While there are other activities that are fulfilling and pleasurable, these are the core activities that I can easily do to keep my tank full. When I give them priority daily, I think better thoughts and I have a better attitude. I have more focus and discipline to fulfill my life purpose and live in my passions.

A Restored Heart

So if you are worn out, stressed out, or at the point of cracking, consider stopping today and following these steps:

1. Decide that the condition of your heart should always be top priority. (Write yourself a note, and post it somewhere you will see it daily.)

2. Know and be aware of the condition of your heart daily. (Maybe at the time when you reflect daily or when you write in your journal.)

3. Know exactly what fills your heart and keeps it healthy. (Make a list.)

4. Be disciplined to do those activities daily. (And when you fail, start again.)

Do not neglect to take care of yourself. It will enhance your capacity to lead well.

Keep Pedaling

When I participated in the RAGBRAI bicycling event in Iowa in July 2013 with my two brothers and our friend, we were amateur riders. The ride covered hundreds of miles as we traveled from one side of the state to the other. The experience challenged me physically and taught me a thing or two about endurance—both in life and leadership.

RAGBRAI Day 1: We were not sure we could make it—53 miles. The maximum I had biked in one day was 40 miles. It was hot, too. Sore and stumbling, we made it. But all four of us wondered about the second day. It would be the longest day of the ride—83 miles! Could we do it? And what about our sore legs?

RAGBRAI Day 2: Our bottoms hurt when we took to the bicycle seats again in the morning. Our quadriceps burned! And by the way, the second day we would climb hills that would total 4000 feet. We thought if we could finish the second day, we could finish the entire week. After all, the third day was mostly flat land.

I don't know how, but after riding all day, at 7:30pm we made it. Ten minutes after we made it, a howling storm that would last about 30 minutes hit our campground. Luckily the group that was carrying our tents had already set them up. So we quickly took cover, and suddenly...hail! As my brother's tent and clothes somehow became fully soaked during the mayhem, we decided to stay at a local hotel in the little town we were in. Since they were completely booked, they let us sleep in their banquet room—with 15 other people. We were thankful, until we discovered that two guys were heavy snorers. It had been one heck of a day, and a night that was not restful. When the third day came, I did not know how we would do it.

RAGBRAI Day 3: As we got on our bikes that morning, I didn't think my muscles would move. But to my surprise, after the first few miles my legs were feeling great, my breathing was on target, and overall I was feeling good. The flat land helped. I was also shocked on the third day to find a pleasant breeze. I had been through so much, so many hills, so many miles the previous evening. I thought it must have been that I was simply getting stronger. Getting better. And I was.

The secret? I kept pedaling. I stuck with it, even in the darkest hour, the worst hill, the severest storm. Even though I still had to be intentional the following days of the ride, it became doable, and at least mentally I knew I could conquer it.

As a leader, it is so hard when we become discouraged. When people leave us, when we don't find the right team, when the culture is failing, or the vision is unclear. When the boss is not understanding and the closest people to us will not come along, it is easy to give up. But I say keep pushing. Keep fighting. Keep advancing. Your muscles will get stronger, and your confidence will grow greater. Your leadership will become better and your impact will become deeper. Keep pedaling, my friend.

Navigate the Hills and Valleys of Leadership

As I made it through the RAGBRAI bicycling ride, I took a lesson from the rolling hills we traversed. Whether on a challenging bicycle ride, or a personal leadership journey, we are going to navigate all sorts of terrain, weather all sorts of changes, and travel miles with all sorts of people. We will find success when we accept change and learn to deal with whatever comes across our paths.

My brothers and friend and I made this trip together—all of us novices. New to cycling, my legs were constantly sore. I watched with keen interest over 15,000 strong riders, mostly 25 to 45 in age. Some were children as young as ten and a handful were in their 70's! One person was on a unicycle and another brought her dog along. As we stopped in each small town, it was phenomenal to experience the local culture and foods and meet the local Iowans that farm that beautiful state.

As I negotiated the Iowa hills among the beautiful cornfields, I had plenty of time to think. Several of the experiences and scenes reminded me of different aspects of leadership. One was the rolling landscape we travel in our leadership journey.

Navigating the Rolling Hills of Iowa

There are three types of terrain: flat land, downhill and uphill. The flat lands were predictable, manageable, and for the most part easy to pedal across. Downhills were a different story. Suddenly, I was an instant success. I mastered it quickly. And as I coasted down I had a chance to relax and enjoy the winds blowing on my face, sometimes up to 37 miles per hour. Usually after a downhill came the uphills, and that's where most cyclists struggle—I was certainly no exception.

After the first few days, I figured out a secret to manage uphills better. I found out that if during the downhill I remained super-focused, I expected the uphill to come. I would then maximize my speed, and as I hit the uphill keep pedaling and downshifting systematically. I got through 70% of most hills on the momentum of the downhill. And the rest was a piece of cake!

Navigating the Rolling Hills of Leadership

As I think back on my experiences navigating leadership, there were definitely flat lands when things were smooth and straightforward, downhills where things were going my way and I started gaining speed. And then came the uphills—the times when things slowed down. To move forward I had to work hard, struggle, and fight just to stay in the game.

When we are traversing the landscape of leadership, this is normal. I first expected Iowa to be flat—at least I hoped it would be. Likewise, I thought navigating leadership would be easy, especially once I had a few years of experience behind me. Once I discovered and expected hills—both in Iowa and in leadership—I started doing better. At least emotionally, I handled the uphills better, not only because I prepared during the downhills, but also because I expected the uphills to come. All of a sudden, I was okay with the challenges because I anticipated them.

And as I engaged the next hill, a part of me wished the entire ride would be flat lands or downhills. But then, I reminded myself that this is the ride I signed up for. That's why most people don't succeed at it, because they are not willing to continually negotiate the recurring hills of Iowa—or leadership! I wanted that final prize. I wanted to participate in the tradition of dipping my front tire in the Mississippi River on the last day. I want the prize of going with great people to great places to accomplish great things.

We will experience every sort of terrain on our journey in leadership. We will navigate it best when we accept the variations and commit to keep pedaling despite the conditions. And when we do, we set ourselves and our teams up to successfully cross the finish line.

Tools

chapter 10

Bonus Tool

10-POINT LEADERSHIP DIAGNOSTIC TOOL

10-Point Leadership Diagnostic Tool

When patients come into my clinic with a medical complaint, I go through a mental checklist to diagnose their condition and provide treatment. For instance, if a 55-year-old male, who is a smoker with high blood pressure and diabetes, comes in with a complaint of chest pain, I first rule out a heart condition, then lung disease, then reflux, arthritis, pain-producing rash, and so on. The same complaint from a healthy 23-year-old evokes a different list of possible causes. After years of training as a doctor, health symptoms naturally trigger an immediate diagnostic checklist in my mind. Years of leadership study and practice have a similar effect on me.

So, let's take a common leadership complaint: *My organization (team, family, church, etc.) is not growing in breadth or depth.*

Would you allow me to be your "leadership doctor" and go through a diagnostic checklist with you? The following 10-point tool can be used to check the symptoms of a multitude of leadership ailments. Let's go through this list together like we would if you came into my clinic with a complaint of chest pain.

1. You are not making time to think.

I place this at the top of the list because I see it as a very common problem with us, as leaders. We become so busy that we just don't make time to do calm, productive thinking. When you let the thrill of action replace the discipline of thinking, you and your organization will be in trouble.

Think alone. Think with others. Just have consistent, relaxed thinking time. Thinking takes tremendous discipline. It requires you to stop and be still. Stopping to think could result in temporary production losses because you may have to pause the action. But in the long run, it will prove to be invaluable toward your overall growth and success. Block time daily or weekly just for thinking.

2. You are experiencing vision problems.

- **The vision is not clear.** So often our vision is fuzzy to us. We know we want to build a great organization. We may want a lot of members or clients, or desire to build a world-class team. Parts of our vision may be clear, but we often fail to produce an endpoint that is clear in its entirety. Friend, clear means simple. Clear means easy to understand and internalize at a gut level. We must be diligent to re-clarify the vision periodically. Vision is like a windshield in changing weather. It tends to fog up often, so we need to turn on the wipers or defrost the glass.

- **The vision is not inspiring.** Your vision must be inspiring to *you* first. Moreover, it must be inspiring to others if you want great people to join and stay with you. Your vision must be grand enough for people to want to be a part of it. Everyone wants to play a role in a success story.

- **You are not dedicated to the vision.** What are you willing to give up to see your vision through? If you're not willing to give up much, the people with you will not either. When you believe in the vision, and give it your heart and dedicated effort, it will come to pass.

- **You are not inviting others to join you.** This is a very common mistake that leaders make. Friend, if the vision is yours alone, then it will be you alone trying to accomplish it. Make *your* vision, *our* vision. Having people buy into your vision rests on two core elements. First, do they buy into you, as the leader? Second, have they been invited to participate in shaping the vision? If the answer is yes to these two questions, your odds of having others come along with you is much higher.

3. You are not bringing the best people along to join you.

If you bring mediocre people to join you—with mediocre skills, mediocre maturity, and mediocre experience—you will have mediocre results. The best teams recruit the best people.

4. Your relationships are poor.

This is a very common symptom of a lack of growth. Building a strong team is dependent on a culture of strong personal (not just professional) relationships. When you consider your coworker a friend, someone you trust, you are much more likely to be creative and productive with them. Healthy relationships begin with the leader. Demonstrate to others how relationships are fostered, maintained, and grown. Then expect it in others.

5. You are not cultivating a culture of growth and training.

Bring the best people on board, then grow them. It is not enough to merely add great people to your team. You must also make a concerted effort to aggressively grow them in every facet possible. Training. Reading. Presenting. Writing. Insist on growth in every area that is applicable to your team. Make sure developing yourself and your people become an expected part of your culture. Not once a year. Not once a month. Constantly and consistently. Do it together. And send them to get training alone, as well. Have them come back and teach you and everyone else what they have learned.

6. You are not consistently communicating with people.

There are so many books on change management. I find all these change principles to be good, but I believe one principle supersedes them all. Communicate. But here is the key. You must maintain a system of communication that is regular and expected. Meet with your team consistently and discuss issues. Leave sensitive matters to be discussed one-on-one, then bring it up in a group discussion. Otherwise, you can lose control with high emotions and debates. I am a proponent of each leader aiming to meet with their team members one-on-one, on a weekly basis. When communication is part of your culture, any growth initiatives or change can be accomplished with so much more ease.

7. You are not creating a culture that values teamwork.

Creating strong teams is the cornerstone of your success. Study teamwork. Read books about it. Practice proven team-building principles. Successful teams are built on cultures of solid relationships between team members. Bringing a team together begins with combining people who have natural harmony, similar values, and work ethics. When leaders bring on the most qualified people without consideration for how they will blend with the team, this rarely works. It's our responsibility as leaders to weigh all these things, hold each member accountable to their roles and relationships among the team. If someone is consistently tearing the team down, we must remove them. It's that important.

8. You have not created scalable systems.

If you have not taken the time to complete the mundane process of defining and refining your processes in a written fashion, you will not grow. Make the time to implement standards and means by which to measure successes or failures. These systems must be applicable and easy to follow.

9. Your business model is poor.

Be practical. The whole premise of your vision and strategy may not be workable. Have the courage to ask whether what you are attempting is actually a good idea. Follow your gut, your intuition, and your heart. Then be brave enough to listen to the naysayers, the realists, and those who tell it like they see it. Let all these things become tools to help you shape a vision that is both inspiring and doable.

10. You are not watching the bottom line.

If your organization is not built on a strong financial foundation, everything can come to a screeching halt. Watch your cash flow. Watch your revenue trends. Don't stick your head in the sand when it comes to the finances. Otherwise, your whole organization will be washed away like a sand castle.

If you are not experiencing the growth you would like, identify which of these symptoms may be contributing to your decline. And begin treating them, just the way you would treat your body back to health. Let's see our teams and organizations thrive!

Endnotes

[1] Tom Rath, *StrengthsFinder 2.0*, (Gallup Press, 1 Edition, February 1, 2007)

[2] Tom Rath, *StrengthsFinder 2.0*, (Gallup Press, 1 Edition, February 1, 2007)

[3] Tony Baron, *The Art of Servant Leadership*, (Wheatmark, Inc., April 11, 2010)

[4] Charles Duhigg, *The Power of Habit: Why We Do What We Do in Life and Business*, (Random House Trade Paperbacks, January 7, 2014 reprint edition).

[5] Charles Duhigg, *The Power of Habit: Why We Do What We Do in Life and Business*, (Random House Trade Paperbacks, January 7, 2014 reprint edition).

[6] Spencer Johnson, M.D., *Who Moved My Cheese?: An Amazing Way to Deal with Change in Your Work and in Your Life*, (G. P. Putnam's Sons, 1 edition September 8, 1998)

[7] Headquarters Department of the Army, *Operations FM 3-0*, (Washington D.C., February 27, 2008)

[8] Tony Schwartz, "Want Productive Employees? Treat Them Like Adults." Harvard Business Review, March 2013. http://blogs.hbr.org/2013/03/treat-employees-with-trust/

[9] Henry Cloud, *Necessary Endings: The Employees, Businesses, and Relationships that All of Us Have to Give Up in Oder to Move Forward*, (Zondervan, January 18, 2011)

[10] Samarnh Pang, "True Friend." Great Inspiring Stories, August 2012. http://lifeaward.blogspot.com/2012/08/true-friend.html

[11] Keith Ready, "Genuine and Caring Leadership." A Gift of Inspiration, January 2008. http://www.agiftofinspiration.com.au/stories/leadership/Genuine.shtml

[12] Clare O'Connor, "American Booty," *Forbes Magazine*, (March 26, 2012)

[13] John Maxwell, *Failing Forward: How to Make the Most of Your Mistakes*, (Thomas Nelson, 1 edition March 8, 2000)